TAKE IT FROM THE TOP

TAKE IT FROM THE TOP

TERRI LYONS

Website: www.nightowl5869.net

This book was printed in the United States of America.

To order additional copies of this book, contact:
Xlibris Corporation
1-888-795-4274
www.Xlibris.com
Orders@Xlibris.com
65791

Introduction

Since the millennium I have found myself reflecting upon a remarkable epoch and baffling changes in American society and the history of the human experience. I'm truly fascinated with the wonders of technology that make the world smaller and effortless communication across every ocean just seconds away.

But I have found the need to harvest the wisdom from the past to counter the side effects of the modern world. My reflections took me to a time when people ate home cooked food and took a nap to cure their maladies. People turned to each other, not pills and electronics to remedy life's trials and tribulations. I reflect upon a time when people were not told what to like and what to eat and how to prepare it. The art of improvisation was an integral part of American culture and manipulative media didn't have such a strong grip on one's mind and body, nor did it waste time with useless news.

Time can erase parts of our history we used to know. Education for consent and concision can make relevant knowledge disappear completely or render it useless. It is in those gaps I called for some nuance and recognition of the pain and brutality people suffered. I need an honest look at the time of soul stirring parties and prayers; savory cuisines; hardy gut splitting laughter and most of all the voice of the spirit through rhythm and sound.

Take it from the Top is a sequel to Let Me Tell You What Mama Said where I began with my mother's young life during The Depression and my great-grandmother who was a slave as a child. I journeyed through her life through WWII when she first came to North Philly, met my father, bought their first home and began their life together with music. Take it From the Top continues that journey. It is just one of many stories from the 1960s an incredible decade filled with memories of my parents and their musical career. I was old enough through part of the era to remember what happened, but needed my mother's complete version to contextualize events and changes.

I found solace in the wisdom and experience of my seniors and humor in their point of view. They lived during a time when having common sense mattered and foolishness simply wasn't tolerated. Problems were worked out one day at a time with endurance and understanding. The last years of upward mobility were a powerful motivator for triumph over poverty into the world of middle class. Take it From the Top is where mama's story continues and my story begins.

1961

The memories of my childhood consist of a time in history when the social environment in America was boiling over with bitter rage and confusion. People of African descent who lived and suffered through the 1960s can testify that it was wrapped up in both delight and terror inundated in feelings of anger, joy and a mission. However, despite what was happening socially and politically, the cabarets were always jumping and music seemed to fuel the revolution and kept the spirits of black folks alive. Churches nourished their broken dreams even as the streets ran with their blood. A new conscious level was beginning to take place among black people whose psyche was stripped raw from the recent horrors of Emmet Till, The Greensboro Four, the bus boycott and the violence suffered during attempts to integrate schools.

Food and liquor was a Saturday night staple and the jailhouses busted at the seams by a people tired, frustrated and disillusioned with a system that was designed to keep them oppressed, subjugated and submissive, making the sixties the most memorable decade in the twentieth century.

I was born in HUP, Hospital of the University of Pennsylvania in West Philadelphia. Mom and dad brought me to our Cobbs Creek home on the 800 block of Cecil Street. It was the best move of its time before the migration to Mount Airy. By the early sixties, the tree lined one-way street was completely filled with young struggling Negro couples. A few families who had cars were parked on one side of the street. My small beautiful world consisted of a barbershop across the street and Manny's store on the corner. Manny sold everything from Johnnie Smokers to cold cuts. The front porch was my outside playground. Patti Labelle lived around the corner on 58th Street. The entire neighborhood was saturated with the aroma of fried porgies or trout, greens and cornbread. Most women were housewives and mothers who kept the porch hot with neighborhood gossip and the latest national upset. My mother and I found ourselves reliving the past more frequently since the millennium. Mom related her memories to me over a cup of coffee.

"Your father and I were so happy to finally be in our own home. We lived in that third floor apartment on 21st Street for ten years. Your father started working at Wyeth Laboratories in 1951 scrubbing the stairs and emptying trash. It was on 12th Street near Washington Avenue, down the street from Dubrows Furniture Store. By 1959 he worked in manufacturing and the company moved to Malvern, PA. That's when we could afford our home.

As a matter of fact; it was the same week my girl Billie Holiday died, July 17th. When you came along, I stayed home and took care of you. And while things appeared to be getting better for most black folks, there was tension in the air and it was building. It seemed to really depend on where you lived. At the time, Cecil Moore was raising hell in North Philly. He knocked that wall down at Girard College and protested against the Mummers using blackface. Cecil Moore fought for poor people who had no voice. Black folks were rising up along with the growth of the Civil Rights Movement and there was a small segment of black people who were starting to thrive and do well for themselves. West Philly was the place to live, especially the south side where we were. For the first time we were getting good jobs and buying nice houses and some folks were just experiencing what it felt like to have two sheets on their bed. But many people were still suffering and it seemed that those who were moving upward in life began to distance themselves from those who were being left behind."

1963

Johnny Carson's *Who Do You Trust* was on television while mom was adding Oxydol to her laundry. Suddenly the TV went blank and mom wondered what the problem was. She thought maybe the picture tube blew or possibly technical difficulties. It was dead for so long she considered calling a neighbor to see if they were having the same problem, but the phone was dead.

Mama told me she became a little nervous with the television and phone out. She refused to believe it at first. She turned the television off, and then turned it on again. The tubes were lit and she saw the blue dot on the screen, but not much else. She juggled the cradle on the phone again and still no dial tone.

Hearing talk from the other neighbors on the front porch on that cold and cloudy November day, she grabbed her jacket and ventured outside. They were complaining about the same problem. Phone conversations had been cut short and people were missing their soaps. Nobody had any answers, but they were relieved to know they weren't alone and tried to assure themselves everything would soon return to normal. Mom came back inside and shook off the cold with a cup of coffee. Later she bundled me up and we both went out to the back yard where she hung the clothes.

A Special Report was the first thing mama saw on television when we came back inside. Walter Cronkite was taking his glasses off and announced to the world that President Kennedy was shot dead in Dallas, Texas. James Tate was the mayor of Philadelphia. Doctor King had just marched on Washington and I was two years old.

Over the years, I heard mama and her friends talk about it all. They talked about the death of Medgar Evers, the four little girls who were bombed at 16th Street Baptist Church and Negroes getting better jobs. They talked about the cabaret last Saturday night at the Imperial Ballroom and the upcoming one at the Adelphi House. They discussed how Esposito's on 9th Street had the best meats and how Piggy's on Ridge Avenue had the best greens. They mentioned the colored person they saw on television and James Brown's big hit *Try Me*. Notes were compared on who was going to be at the next house party, who cooked the best ribs and who wore the sharpest clothes. Happy to be out of the south, some black folks weren't particularly interested in integration. They didn't need or want anybody telling them how to live or how to have a good time. They were busy enjoying a culture that wasn't contaminated by unwanted intervention.

Colored folks, as African Americans were called at the time, were being bombed and attacked by police dogs in the south. As their blood gushed onto the streets of America, tempers were flaring in many parts of the country. Black folks were being jailed and lynched at alarming rates because they wanted to exercise the rights that the United States Government claimed every American had. The north was plagued with riots and marches as well. Blacks residing in California endured random attacks from police and had no recourse for self defense.

Doctor King was hated by some whites and spurned by some colored folks who were terrified of the white man's wrath. And yet, in the eye of this storm, black owned businesses boomed, churches stomped and dance halls rocked with a certain pride and pain that wasn't apart of the rest of America. Marches and sit-ins it seemed wouldn't produce a population of brotherhood; instead, it only provoked the rulers of this country to neutralize what it couldn't control. Many Negroes believed ignorance had more power than consciousness. Others believed white folks couldn't be made to accept them as equal partners in America. The Supreme Court could not outlaw a racist mind. Contempt and resentment left whites and coloreds wondering if this integration thing was really worth it. White folks were often violent toward peaceful protesters, but were in dire need of protection when black folks retaliated.

Marginalization from the larger society created a special kind of freedom black folks enjoyed. We had our own social customs of loving and fussing. We weren't inhibited when we prayed and partied. Raw truth in all of its beauty and ugliness was openly owned by most. Besides, integration has nothing to do with equality anyway. Nobody cried integration—they cried freedom. That's what it was really about; equality, respect and freedom, freedom from the subjugation of demagogues.

I grew up when Gimbels had the Thanksgiving Day parade in Philadelphia. All movie theaters had ushers armed with a flashlight to guide movie goers to their seat. All night movies like the Studio and the Center was where people cuddled up for the night. It was the only air conditioned refuge during the pre-mall era. Liquor bottles had green government seals and Coke a Cola came in green bottles. Esso and American were the major gas stations. They featured super leaded gas called high test and issued S&H green stamps. A uniformed gas station attendant filled the tank, checked the oil and washed the windshields. There were only American made cars on the road and they didn't have anti-lock brakes, air bags or air conditioning—just A.M. radio.

Fridays were fish day because it was the cheapest food to buy. Pick-up trucks had a scale hanging on the back and traveled up and down the street selling everything from vegetables to fish to eggs. My mother was in line with the other ladies to get fresh fish for Friday night dinner. Some trucks were loaded with sheets and redwood painted porch furniture.

Before plastic and recycled materials took over the world everything was made of real metal and wholesome wood. Even pine seemed to be of better quality. Back then there were no recalls, guarantees or warranties to be harassed into buying because everything was built to last and it did. Some stuff was passed down through the family or the neighborhood. Everything from market carts to vacuum cleaners was metal and sturdy. They were bought once and they lasted forever. Strollers were made of metal with vinyl seats and sometimes a canvas hood that flipped back and forth. It didn't collapse with the child still inside. Playpens and cribs were made of sturdy wood with metal hinges and no child met their death trapped inside them.

Having a television was a novel experience because it only happened once and furniture was attentively wrapped in custom plastic. Walls were adorned with starburst clocks and a blond hair, blue eyed Jesus in nearly every household in Philadelphia. Screens replaced storm sashes every spring behind single pane windows. When a thunderstorm popped up everyone stopped what they were doing and went inside to sit down.

Television and lights were turned off and people got off the phone. No activity was allowed whatsoever, not even talking. Everyone sat perfectly still until the storm passed and patiently let the Lord do His works. People didn't have to be told about the dangers of lightning. It wasn't called safety awareness. Nobody needed pamphlets and seminars. It was called common sense to get out of the way of bad weather. It wasn't discussed. It was done.

Mama looked back on a time that was turbulent, but not complicated. We sat at the kitchen table, forty years after the death of Doctor King sharing our memories of the past. She filled me in on everything I was too young to remember. She remembered when banks offered six percent tax free interest on every passbook savings account and Roosevelt stamps were six cents each. Every bank customer got their coins counted for free. It was old school customer service. I remembered when my dad put snow tires on our car every winter; better yet, chains after the storm. People referred to the bitter cold wind as the "Hawk". Howard Johnson's Restaurants monopolized the Pennsylvania Turnpike and White Tower hamburgers had all of Broad Street.

American Bandstand aired from the Arena at 46th and Market and the Wagner Ballroom located at Broad and Old York Road were popular white teenage hangouts. Beverages came in glass bottles and nothing was tamper proof. Every morning either Abbott or Sealtest milk was at the front door next to a sack of Stork diapers. Long distance calls had to be connected through an operator on black rotary phones rented from Bell of Pennsylvania, known as Ma Bell. The gas man yelled out house numbers on his way down the street checking meters and trash was collected twice a week. Garbage was picked up sometime during the night and mail was delivered twice a day. Supermarkets closed at 10p.m., malls didn't exist and nothing except restaurants were open on Sunday.

1964

Mom used to walk behind me as I peddled my shiny red tricycle with red, white and blue streamers on the handle bars up and down the sidewalk. She met with the other mothers who were doing the same with their children. Some had babies over their shoulder; others had the rest of their brood trailing behind them. The porch ladies were on patrol all day long. Ms. Ruth, Ms. Doris, Ms. Lorraine and another lady who always had bright pink rollers in her hair huddled on first one porch then another. They knew who went in or came out from everyone's house. They knew what time the men left for work, the truth about daddy's maybe and who had their head hanging out of the window. They greeted everyone on the sidewalk below begging their pardon for a moment of their time. Their voices were just above a whisper talking to mom about Ms. Loretta across the street that hopped the banister all day gathering news, like bees gathering pollen, and spread it to the other receptive neighbors. The latest news was that Ms. Loretta's home was in desperate need of soap and water. It had caught fire the other day from one of her seven wild ass kids playing with matches. Her oldest son was in trouble again. He was supposed to be a member of a gang called The Creek. Cool Earl and Cornbread which was spray painted everywhere were probably some of his friends. The lady with the bright pink rollers in her hair said that boy has a job printing license plates. Her pink head bopped back and forth when she started talking about Ms. Dorothy. Bright Pink was forever telling people what they should and shouldn't do and cussed people out behind their back. She had a little too much to say about Ms. Dorothy's husband. Ms. Loretta went back and told Ms. Dorothy what Bright Pink said.

Ms. Dorothy knocked on Bright Pink's door and cussed her out and offered her to the street for an official beat down. The porch ladies hashed that over before Bright Pink showed up. They said she was lucky Dorothy wasn't one of those lye slinging mamas. I could only suppose my mother would be the next topic after we left. "She think she cute with her ugly self. I can't stand the heifer. She don't know, I coulda had her man, but I didn't want him," Bright Pink assured the porch ladies.

I heard my mother say "Did you know that Willie just bought a car? I know Barbara must be on cloud nine." Bright Pink cut mom a look and said "I don't know why, she can't drive it. Not like some people I know; driving a big car with nobody in it but them." That's when I learned what signifying meant. Mom cut her right back with just a little bass in her voice and said, "What I do with my car ain't nobody's business unless they paying the note." I felt a flash of heat crawl over my entire body. I escaped up the street on my red hot ride as mom went on with the ladies. My short lived freedom came to an abrupt end when mom caught my handle bars on my return down the street and guided me toward our front porch. I wasn't much more than a toddler, but I remember that day. Mom filled in the rest for me. Mom said "They were just like that mess up in Ambler. Fussing and fighting about something that's none of their business or over some man that didn't want either one of them. Always up in somebody's business and half the time they didn't know what they were talking about. They were just running their mouth. The next thing you know everybody's mad. A couple of the ladies were okay sometimes because they kept me laughing.

But I'm telling you stay away from idle-minded people with nothing better to do than cut down other people. My friends were busy people and lived out of the neighborhood." Mom mocked the ignorance and pettiness that I told her was still prevalent.

Every year brought ladies with swollen bellies who drank and smoked and dined on lots of fish, chitterlings, fatback, biscuits, lima beans, neck bones and greens. They gave birth to eight and nine pound babies who still managed to be healthy. I remember most of them with sponge rollers in their hair or tight hot iron curls. They wore gingham house dresses in every color with one bra strap midway down their forearm and accessorized with a cloth diaper over the shoulder. Most gave birth at Mercy Douglass on Woodland Avenue, known as the colored hospital of the city or Philadelphia General Hospital, PGH, nicknamed the Philly Slaughter House. The mouse-infested hospital had wards with ten to fifteen people in one room. Hospital stays averaged ten days to two weeks after having a baby. It wasn't a drive-thru service courtesy of managed health care. Newborns were almost two weeks old before they arrived home for the first time wearing Birds Eye diapers and rubber pants. Nurses wore white uniforms with white stockings and white shoes. Her white cap represented her nursing school. When Frank Rizzo, nicknamed The Cisco Kid, became mayor the free for all hospital was torn down.

The summer of 1964 was known as Freedom Summer. Mom and dad talked about it every so often. Colored folks couldn't vote down south and some white college students from the north were supposed to go down there and help to straighten it out. Sometimes mom and dad talked like they were angry, but they weren't arguing. My mother's church in Penllyn, Pennsylvania was under construction from a Ku Klux Klan attack and my father's family in Durham, North Carolina was in the grip of Jim Crow. They talked about non violent organizations; SNCC, SCLC and CORE standing up to the white man. Many of them were jailed and beaten time and again. I heard some of it before. I was on the porch playing jacks a few days earlier with two little girls who lived down the street from me. Their parents were talking about it too. We were trying to make up our minds if we were Negro or colored. We figured Negroes were from up here, coloreds were from down south and therefore we didn't have to worry about being beaten or bombed.

I loved warm afternoons. Doors and windows stayed open welcoming a gentle breeze throughout the house and playtime was much longer. Mom saved most Wednesdays for her and me. She packed a couple of sandwiches and Frank's orange soda and took me to Cobbs Creek Park or to Children's Day at Valley Forge Music Fair which was a tent at the time. Other times we took afternoon strolls up 52nd Street. She'd stop by Payees Shoe Store and Woolworth or to King James Records. When she couldn't afford the three dollar album, she bought the 45 record for fifty cents. As she learned the lyrics she sang to me and danced with me and sometimes we sang together.

Mom said "Buying records was something else at that time. Albums came out sometime after The War, but 45s had just come out in the late fifties. People didn't have a lot of records because most didn't have a record player or Hi-Fi. The old folks were still used to the old shellac 78's and the gramophone. Your father started buying albums and everybody wanted to borrow them. Of course he never saw most of them again. AM radio was most popular, but I liked to listen to 96.5FM. It was a jazz station. Sid Mark was the deejay. He started his show with the song *Folks on the Hill*. That station was where I heard Della Reese's *Good Morning Blues* and Lionel Hampton's *Stardust* which was recorded live in Pasadena around 1945. He played all of the greats. We had just bought a Hi-Fi at Frank and Cedars' department store and I couldn't wait to get to buy my records and come home to play them."

Dad had his nine to five and on the side he played guitar and gigged around in what was known as the Chitlin Circuit. He played from one place to another as almost every musician did. His travels brought him to a group of guys. George Glover, Hardy Hall, Freddie Walker called "Peanut" and Ray Carter were in a group called the Upstarts. They gigged around throughout Philadelphia and Chester, PA. Dad played with Freddie the Freeloader and Charlie Chisholm bands. Finally he met up with Mickey Collins and started to gig with him as a side man. Mickey, older than dad, was an all around entertainer. His shtick kept people hot. He played drums and sang. Sometimes he had two bands performing in different locations on the same night.

Dad performed with Mickey at Friday or Saturday night cabarets and sometimes mom went along. From the start it was looked down on by my grandmother, Nana and her sister, Aunt Bert. My aunt and grandmother were from the old school where a black woman's ambition went no further than the white folk's kitchen and keeping an immaculate house. They scorned night life and *that* music. My grandmother had nothing but contempt for women who wore make-up although she sometimes wore it herself. They made sure mom had her share of grief. They disdained iniquitous activities mom had no chance of escaping as long as she was apart of night life. They thought she was destined for hell unless she sought Jesus and found satisfaction in stirring gravy and whipping potatoes for the rest of her life.

Mom thought they should pay her bills if they were so worried about it. Mom was a country girl at heart, but she had enough wisdom to keep trouble away. She often told me this world is filled with the devil and the angel and life will give you a chance to play with both of them, but she also wanted to break the boredom of clean, safe living and put a few dollars in her pocket. Weekend cabarets were looked forward to by most people to break away from the dirt and stress of the week. There was a certain freedom that went along with the night life and mama couldn't resist it. She was drawn in by the music. She loved the people. Mom and dad were just beginning a new career and were on their way to a delightful time.

Dad with Mickey Collins Band, 1955

Cabaret

Mickey Collins, Henry Carter and Charlie Gains were the most popular bandleaders in Philadelphia and had the city sewn up. While with Collins, dad had the opportunity to work with Patti Labelle and the Blue Bells at Rosedale Beach in Delaware and with Music Associates. Dad began to work with various social organizations that were emerging all over the Delaware Valley. He met members from various social clubs such as the Continentals, the Guardsmen and the Amicitia Club. He met choreographers Marion Cuyjet, Jerome Gaymon and the great Eugene Raymond Jones. Mom and Jerome became lifelong friends. Mister Jerome was a sporting life man who took mom and dad around to make connections. It was through him that dad's band eventually became the top pick for the annual Cotillion and, in part how mom and dad began to meet and mingle with different groups of people. The ladies weren't regular mommies and housewives. They were, well, different. Most of them had jobs.

They were dressed up and wore make-up all the time. Some were college educated. They spoke differently and laughed with restraint. They smelled of perfume and didn't have a lot of children, some had no children. A few of them lived in big houses with a fireplace. The ladies served cocktails and hot snacks they called hors d'oeuvres. The men didn't have regular jobs. They had positions or owned their own business. They didn't have to wear a uniform to work and they belonged to Greek organizations. Mom had to go shopping.

Philadelphia Transportation Company, known as P.T.C., had green and white trolleys and buses. The 34 trolley stopped at 58th Street right across from Food Fair Supermarket. We stood where "Cool Breeze" was sprayed on a wall behind us. The subway surface trolley brought us to City Hall. I loved the hustle of the city. We walked east on Market strolling through Wanamaker's. Mom and I shared delicious treats from the candy counter near the eagle. Sometimes she bought chocolate coins wrapped in gold foil for me. We stood with the crowd waiting for the elevator. I watched the doors open like magic. A uniformed man stepped aside announcing whether the elevator was local or express. After mom and I stepped onto the elevator the man in the blue uniform closed the door, pulled a gate and turned the wheel. He announced each floor all the way up. You had to answer him with the same number for him to stop. Mom hollered nine. He put on the brakes—turned the wheel, unlocked the gate and opened the door to let us out. Our first stop was the ladies room which was lined with pay toilets. Ladies held the stall door open for the next person in line to use. That saved everybody from having to piss away a dime. We went to the department where mom bought lovely buttermilk Dorothy Grey soap and then scooted to the other side where mom paid her bill. Finally, we dined at the Crystal Room.

After lunch, we browsed among the bustling crowd, in and out of stores making our way to Lit Brothers and Gimbels department stores. That was where mom began to expand her wardrobe of gowns and cocktail dresses. We passed by Snellenburg. Horn & Hardhart was filled with tasty steam table lunches. It had a large clock on the wall with no numbers. Skid row bums came in scavenging leftover food. In front of Reading

Terminal was where I first saw Hari Krishna. They wore white sheets and had bald heads, except for a patch of hair on top of their head. Banging tambourines and barefoot, they jumped up and down in some kind of foreign chant seeking spare change. They scared me. Mom never told me anything about them. She just yanked my arm for me to keep walking. I don't think she really knew herself except to leave them alone and go on her way. She was trying to get next door and down the steps to enter Arrow's Men's Store to buy daddy's shirts. From there we moved on to Sun Ray Drug Store to load up on dad's favorite deodorant, Right Guard and her must have cold cream, Lady Esther. Sometimes we walked from Market Street to Chestnut Street where there were a variety of shoe stores. Mom's favorite was Baker Shoe Store and Chandlers. Every pair of shoes had to match her outfit and if it didn't, she had the shoes dyed. A couple of high end stores such as Nan Duskin and The Blum Store were only for window shopping.

Skid row was located around 9th and Race where winos and street bums had a home. They used to stay in the movie house called The New Garden Movie somewhere around 8th Street and Vine. It was known as the "Scratch House" because many of those bums had lice. The closest we had to a homeless shelter was a flophouse. Mom said she never saw families, just liquored up men. Phone booths were as plentiful as bus stops. Closing the collapsible door turned a light on automatically and sometimes a ventilation fan. To place a call was ten cents. Deposit slots were above the rotary for nickels, dimes and quarters. The old booths had wooden seats and the newer ones were aluminum and home to the street bums. They were up and down Market Street begging for money and gathering cigarette butts. Their appearance gave me the creeps. They looked awful and some smelled worse. Mama told me for the most part they were harmless. These were people who were down on their luck and maybe a little sick in the head. It's the clean cut man in the expensive suit with the briefcase I should be worried about. They'll steal what you have and ever hope to make. Mom would give the black bums some money and a cigarette sometimes, but not the white ones. She mumbled something about them being free all of their life—"I ain't free yet" she complained to herself.

The site of the majestic Earle Theater became the Grant Store at 11th and Market. On occasion I enjoyed a hot dog and a side order of French fries in the plastic basket at the lunch counter. Milk shakes were made in tall aluminum cups and sodas came from a jerk. I hated the paper straws because they always stuck together. Mom reminded me to keep my fingers from wandering under the table because it was peppered with discarded gum. She shopped for domestic knick knacks that sold for as little as fifty cents—all genuine glass. Westmore make-up came in three shades of white and Cutex nail polish was frosted pink or pearl. Black women used make-up to lighten their skin. Powders and liquids left inexperienced women with light faces and dark necks. A face to the hand in a "shut ya mouth" expression showed a puzzling contrast that left me wondering why black ladies had light, cake batter faces when they dressed up. I enjoyed our Market Street walk back toward City Hall to catch the 34 back home. Sometimes mom let me get a package of peanut butter crackers from the Lance vending machine in the concourse. It kept me quiet and happy as we headed home for dinner.

Warm smells from the kitchen met the evening sun glaring through the living room window. I heard Sam Cook's *A Change is Gonna Come* playing from somewhere outside and competing with the clamor of pots and pans. I sat by the window waiting for dad to come home from work. He worked with penicillin and wore a white uniform that had a peculiar odor I'll never forget. He picked me up high in the air and brought me down with a kiss and the best hug. He held me up to the sink and helped me wash my hands while mom set the table. She pulled the lever on the aluminum ice tray and added the cubes to a pitcher of fresh squeezed lemonade. At six p.m. dad blessed the table for our evening meal consisting of meat or fish with a starch and vegetables served hot and prepared from the kitchen stove. There were no phone calls during mealtime nor talking with a full mouth or elbows on the table. I was taught to ask permission to be excused when I completed my meal. Dessert was homemade cake, Jell-O—or custard. She took the time to cook it all. It was the best treat because it was made with her love. The Good Humor truck was a welcome sight, but not something I was always allowed to have just because I wanted it. All treats were rationed and with a full belly from a solid dinner the desire often wasn't there. Mom and dad took time to ask me about my day. They always talked to me. I was excited to tell dad about my day. I couldn't wait to tell him about a game or a new word I learned from watching Romper Room or a fantastic work of art I created on my etch-a-sketch.

Sometimes I was allowed to watch the Flintstones unless breaking news about the latest riot came on. I knew when it was bad. I was sent to the TV to turn it up while mom and dad sat in stone silence, slowly nodding their head from left to right, occasionally looking at each other. They stopped chewing their food and stared at a film clip of shocking news. They watched marchers being gathered up and singing on their way to jail. They saw protesters tear gassed. Another time a freedom rider bus was bombed. I sat with them watching hundreds of unarmed black people beaten to a bloody pulp trying to register to vote. I stared at them staring; a little upset only because they were. I saw that worried look in their eye and felt that uneasy silence that told me something was wrong, but the details went over my head. I just wanted to see the Flintstones.

I talked to mom about what I remembered when we were looking at *Eyes on the Prize.* The events of the film now forty years old left an indelible mark on my childhood memory. I remembered the grown folks talking about a rally at a church or some kind of melee in the streets. I remembered the police driving "The Red Car" with sirens cutting through humid nights and people being upset or angry about the police or some other violent outbreak. I told mama I still remembered the phone number for the police. Before 911, the number for the police was 2313131. It was the first phone number mama taught me even before our house number. Mom was always there to put it in perspective for me.

I woke up this morning with my mind on freedom

"The country was going through something. The Warren Report had just come out about President Kennedy. There was a lot of suspicion around his death, especially after Lee Harvey Oswald was killed. We really believed the FBI would never lie. Ain't that something? Young folks wasn't trying to hear anything about non—violence, especially up here. Police were beating people upside the head. Cops could harass them in the street for nothing and provoke them into retaliating. It gave the excuse the cops needed to beat, shoot and throw them in jail. Three men from the Freedom Riders were missing the entire summer. Everybody knew they were dead. In some places drugs were getting bad. I heard it called heron and horse. Some of our boys came back from war strung out on heroin. The Vietnam War was getting bigger. Mostly white college kids protested against the war. Negroes had their own war. Then the gangs were popping up. Rival gangs were rumbling in the street. They started stealing antennas from peoples' cars to make zip guns. It was scary sometimes. It was just like during WWII. They were hard times too—men going to war and we were still feeling the Depression. But you know the hard times brought the best good time and the best music. We had good food and drank belly loads of liquor. We didn't kill each other either. Otis Redding, Marvin Gaye and Junior Walker helped us to cope with our trouble. They could tear it up until it made no sense at all!"

Mama told me the porch ladies were full of gossip, but they took good care of their children and other people's too. They didn't have much of anything except pots of stew and a strong belief in one another that no one would harm anyone's child. They fed, loved and reprimanded any child in the neighborhood who got out of hand and it was welcomed by parents. Sometimes, after a neighbor told the parent, the child got it again when they got home. This was before some expert proposed that it couldn't be done that way anymore. Civil law reigned and the comfort of solidarity meant there was no need for anyone to tell these folks how to handle their families.

The pile at the end of the dial!

Summer evenings were filled with the local black AM station playing from somebody's Hi-Fi. The tiny sound of transistor radios could be heard wherever there were teenagers. The Rhythm and Blues stations were located near the right end of the AM band and after the sun went down so did the reception. The big girls spent a lot of time tightening up on their dance steps. They were the only ones allowed to play in the street. When their favorite song came on the radio they turned it up and broke out in the Philly Slop or the Jerk. Small children played under the watchful eye of mothers who were perched on the front porch talking grown folks talk along with some old folks who had nothing better to do. Some kids kept Manny's Store going all day long buying candy cigarettes and shoestring licorice.

I played on my porch with two little girls from up the street who were just a little older than me. We did hand claps to Patty Cake and Miss Mary Mack. We had other rhymes we said to each other for no reason at all. If someone said "guess what" without a thought, anybody could respond with "chicken butt, run around and lick it up!"

Once in a while I was allowed to hit the sidewalk without mom if an older girl was with me. The big girls taught the little ones how to jump Double Dutch. I was double handed at first and couldn't jump Irish at all. Red Light, Green Light and Hopscotch kept us occupied until the street lights came on. Beyond a skinned knee stained with mercurochrome, as we played there was never any imminent danger.

Sometimes mama enjoyed talking to our next door neighbor Ms. Ruth. Ms. Barbara lived on the other side of Ms. Ruth who was on our front porch. They got in a heated discussion about the latest news. I had to stay close by mom to make it easier for her to keep and eye on me. The late afternoon sun reflected on the windows turning them into panes of flashlights.

Ms. Barbara said "Hazel, you know they found those Freedom Boys. I couldn't . . ."

Ms. Ruth cut Ms. Barbara off and began to preach. She said "I knew them boys was dead. I'm *from* Mississippi—Gulf Port. I know them crackers and how they do. See, they take you out in the middle of the night. Ain't no night like a Mississippi night—black up on top of black. Them nasty white folks traveled in herds tracking down niggras—that's what they called us. They dump'em in the river or string'em on a tree. Sometimes they even burn'em. You ever smell flesh burning? Turn your blood ice cold. They wore sheets by night and a police uniform by day—same people! Them F.B.I. people got sheets too I betcha. You know they wasn't gonna let'em live."

Mama was finally able to get a word in "Ain't that something. Put me in mind of Emmett Till. I'll never forget that picture in Jet magazine. Nobody will go to jail for what they did to that boy. And those kids trying to go school in Little Rock a few years back. Lawd bless them people down there. And it looks like all hell is breaking loose everywhere. I never heard of so much carrying on in my life. We're going to go up in one big puff of smoke. No wonder we all got high blood. Dr. King is in jail too I heard."

Ms. Ruth nodded her head and said "They got the kids in jail now. My folks are still there. My mother said the Ofays are frothing at the mouth. She heard something about these Freedom schools they startin. Then there's something about a new party, a black democratic party they startin up. They're trying to get black people to vote. She won't have nothing to do with voting. She's too old for this mess. I want her to pack it up and come with me and Bill. Sometimes I wonder where this is all going to end."

Mom uncrossed her legs and adjusted her butt cheeks then crossed them back again on the porch glider. I was sitting on the middle cushion next to her trying my best to make the glider go faster. The fury in their voice was familiar to me. Almost anytime grown people were talking they seemed to be angry about something. "We'll be dead before it's over. Just look at what we have up here in the land of milk and honey. We can't go to some hotels and restaurants, but I'm not going to worry with it but so much. It's too dangerous. I don't know what these white folks are trying to prove" Mom said.

They were interrupted by the Good Humor bell. I watched how the street cleared in one second flat by kids running home to ask for money to get an ice cream cone. Mom went in the house and gave me a single stick orange Popsicle. The sun was leaving the porch windows and the children had settled on different porches and steps licking away. The ladies resumed their conversation.

"I know what you mean Hazel. We can't let this mess get in our way" Ms. Ruth butted in again. "The cops have a good time whipping anybody's behind and you don't hear any talk about that. But at the same time these Negroes out here need to stop all this carrying on. It's getting to be too much. Now these gangs are starting to act up. That won't do nothing but give the cops another reason to put the Billy club to their head and nothing can be said about it."

Ms. Barbara whispered "You know that's what happened to Loretta's boy. He was out there carrying on with that no good gang The Creek. They tried to rob a grocery store. The cops got'em and beat their brains in on the way to the precinct. Now he got ten years and a busted head. If he was down the road with those boys, he would be swinging from a tree somewhere, how about it Ruth?"

"You don't know evil until you been to Mississippi. I could never understand how people could be so cruel to other people and call it right. Some bible belt that is" Ms. Ruth seemed to be talking to herself as much as Ms. Barbara and my mom.

Mama looked at me and said "I think you've heard enough. It's upsy daisy for you."

Then she turned to Ms. Ruth and Ms. Barbara and said "I'll be back, I have to put this one to bed."

Ms. Ruth said "Take your time Hazel. I got to get mine in the tub. I'll be back out later after the mice are in bed. Night night sweetie."

Ms. Ruth kissed me goodbye and Ms. Barbara waved as everyone made their way home. The street lights were just coming on.

The street grew quiet as mothers gathered their brood at days end and plopped them in the tub. Gurgling drains could be heard from the sewer vent outside. After my Lifebuoy bath, mom always had a nice treat for me. She prepared custard, ice cream or a small slice of cake. Sometimes mom and dad tucked me in together after my piggy back ride upstairs. They read bedtime stories to me or just made one up. They kissed me good night and each other too. Outside my window was a gaslight that gently burned in the back alley and caste a soft glow in my room. Sometimes I heard dad softly strumming his guitar in the dining room while the crickets were waking up. I smelled remnants of Carnation dishwashing liquid and heard the careful clacking of dishes. I heard the ladies at the door. They convened on the porch under the bluish white street lights partially blocked by maples leaves that gently whisked with the slightest breeze. They talked about the latest gossip or the latest news. Their low comforting murmur and an occasional laugh along with the soft squeak of the porch glider put me fast asleep.

Suspicious eyes started early sneering at women who had fewer children or who were anointed with attentive husbands. The porch ladies rocked back and forth with a twisted mouth mumbling about what they thought they knew about the little princess—what she probably thought about others and what she must have thought about herself. It made the air thick with innuendos of jealousy and eye rolls. Mama caught some heat when she threw me in the back seat of our car and left them sitting there. Their gaze went right down the street with us as mom pulled away.

"It's an idle person's job to be worried with what other people do. Some of them didn't see their husbands until he was tired, broke or drunk. Then he was ready to start something. She's mad because he's not doing right by her. He's mad with a house full of kids he sometimes didn't want. He had his personal daily misery just being a black man. Either he couldn't find a job, or had shit for pay all of which was supposed to go to caring for the ever increasing family. Nothing ever seemed to get better. Black men stayed mad with Mister Charlie and then we'd cut each other down. Since he couldn't escape for real he escaped in a dream at the bar or in the arms of another woman. Then, of course, it could be he was just plain no damn good just like his daddy. Some were more than just no account; they were plain nuts. They beat their wives, chased the kids out of the house and raised all kinds of hell keeping everyone upset. Then there were others who behaved themselves, lived nicely and minded their own business. Those were the ones the porch hens didn't like. If you hang around people with a miserable life, you'll soon have one too. They'll see to that" said momma.

My mama told me . . . You better shop around

Back then just about everyone ran a credit book at the corner store that was owned by a white man who happened to be Jewish. He was stocked with cold cuts, canned goods and the best dill pickles in a barrel for a nickel. And for some reason, the Jew was even more loathsome than other white people. Many black folks accused him of over pricing the merchandise and entering an additional higher price into the credit book. The porch ladies reminded each other to look behind the scale when meat was being weighed. They wanted to make sure a thumb wasn't adding another two pounds on the grocery bill. Some suggested telling the butcher to step back from the scale to assure they weren't being cheated. It had the familiar ring of tenant farming, easy credit rip off and predatory lending where the bill was never paid in full no matter how hard one worked or how much they sacrificed. Sounds more like the American way to me. As the times change so does the name, becoming more insidious with every generation, but be assured it is the same game. The porch ladies talked about it all of the time and the dialogue grew angrier with each conversation.

I remember sitting on the porch one day playing jacks. Mom was squeaking on the porch glider sewing in a zipper on the back of her sleeveless top and Ms. Ruth was on her porch with a big jar of Dixie Peach doing her daughter Diane's hair. A short brown skinned woman with big dimples lived up the street. She had one of those behinds that sat up on her back with hips that took a life of their own, almost like wings. She had a strange dance as she sauntered down the street. High Hips were all that came across my mind as I watched her come towards our porch. She greeted everyone with a big smile. "Hey Hazel! How yuh Doing Ruth!" My mom and Ms. Ruth looked up with a smile and said at the same time, "Hi Lorraine!" So that's her name I thought to myself. She was still High Hips to me. My mother asked Ms. Lorraine "Where are you coming from?" Ms. Lorraine ruffled through her shopping bag and said "I just picked up my dress from the Dress Shop on 52nd Street. I'm ready for the cabaret at the Tropical Garden this Saturday night. I got my shoes dyed too!"

Mom said "You're going to be at the Tropical Garden? I'll see you there. Bobby Felder's band from Washington D.C. will be there. I'm getting my hair done Friday. It's going to be something else. I'm going to be at my friends table. We're going to start cooking tomorrow."

Mom spent all week getting her outfit together. I saw her iron her gloves last night. Friday was her day to go to Bailey's head shop on Lombard Street in South Philly. Ms. Lorraine sat down next to Ms. Ruth who asked "So tell me about this dress." Ms. Lorraine pulled out a sleeveless blue chiffon tent dress with a rhinestone collar. The dress was wrapped in tailor shop plastic. Then she pulled out her shoes that were the exact same color with rhinestone buckles. She had a small purse to complete the outfit. They called it the "Total Look".

Ms. Lorraine continued by saying "This dress was in the window for twenty dollars. I had my eye on it for a long time. You know the sales lady Mrs. Silvergold with a heavy accent? She said to me 'come, come you a nice goil. I'll let you have it for fifteen.'"

Mom and Ms. Ruth were cracking up laughing. Ms. Lorraine went on "But I was able to get it down to twelve. I jewed her down real good."

Mama said "So *you* think. It probably wasn't worth more than that to begin with. I bet they got that dress whole sale in New York for five dollars." Meanwhile the lady with those pink rollers was sauntering up the street with a mouth full of Chiclets. She spoke to everyone and sat on the banister swinging her right leg.

Ms. Ruth said "You gotta watch Ms. Silvergold. Sometimes she'll cheat you outta your change. I caught her doing that when I got my Easter hat from her. You know she and her husband have apartments over in North Philly. My sister lives in there. She burns up in the summer and damn near freezes to death in the winter. She comes over here to bathe to keep icicles off her ass. She called him when something needed fixin and never heard a word. Some of those places are about to fall down. He strolls up there fat and proud when it's time to collect the rent, wearing that big pinky ring and rolls off in a big Cadillac car!" Bright Pink and High Hips fell out laughing.

Ms. Ruth was tugging away at her daughter's hair. She had a big wad of grease on the back of her palm. She made a part on Diane's head with the small teeth of the comb and gently massaged the grease in the part. Mom broke the thread with her teeth. I was on my foursies. Mom spoke up "I saw a coat in there I liked once, but it was too high.

Then I saw the same coat on Market Street for five dollars less. You know the Silvergolds own the butcher shop on the corner too. They own a lot of businesses."

"You mean Tillie's, the grocery store on Washington Avenue?" Bright Pink wondered.

"Naw, they're Slavic or something like that. She's talking about the meat store across the street from them" Ms. Ruth said.

"Oh I know which one you mean. I can't think of the name" Ms. Lorraine clapped.

"Tillie's aren't Slavic, they're Sicilian. They're alright. I've been in there. Their prices are reasonable. It's that dress shop and the meat store you got to watch. They will cheat you!" Mom and Ms. Ruth nodded in agreement.

Bright Pink butted in "I know you don't go in that meat store! High as they are? You can get the same thing at Food Fair and have change."

Ms. Ruth put barrettes in Diane's shiny long braids. Diane jumped the banister to my porch and began to play jacks with me.

"Yeah, but I think the meat is better. I get to pick just what I want and how I want it cut. I hate that supermarket meat wrapped in plastic. Just something about it don't set right."

Bright Pink interjected "That's why they fat enough to kill now. They make their money here, renting these apartments, charge sky high prices and living where we can't. When you catch'em cheatin they act like you did something wrong."

A car radio blaring *Stubborn Kind of Fellow* raced down the street. Mom nodded her head "Yeah. And we're paying their mortgage. That's why I like to either go into town or the thrift shops. If I can't afford it, I'll put it on lay away. I like South Philly for my meats. Esposito's beats them all to me. Their meat is fresh and tender and it doesn't cost so much."

As they discussed white people, they were splitting them up into assorted varieties. According to them some cheat, others kill and none were to be trusted. They called some white folks Slavic, a few were called Irish and others were called Jews, but all white people were called Gray and black people were called Blue. As I listened, I wondered to myself what to call the white folks that beat up those colored people I saw on television.

Years later I understood that being Jewish wasn't necessarily the problem. They were no better or worse than anybody else. Jewish people endured their own hellish nightmare and felt the sting of hatred as much as anybody else. They allied with other justice seeking people who were redlined out of neighborhoods and demonized. Jews who chose not to deny their heritage often taught at black colleges because they weren't accepted to teach at white colleges. Their white skin was associated with other white skin that controlled, lied and otherwise abused with impunity, a voiceless population that made Jews a target of anger as well. No matter where any white skinned individual originated, it was understood by most black people that they were being exploited because they were thought to be ignorant and powerless. They were also expected to submit to what others thought they should be and to internalize it as their own.

When combined with everything else that was wrong in America, the constant cheating, the imposed ignorance, the police brutality, the joblessness, the shitty schools, the poverty and a general condition of helplessness ignored and perpetuated by "The Establishment", it's no wonder many stores were later burned and looted during the riots(unless Soul Brother was painted on the door). The porch ladies said the local police destroyed the Soul Brother businesses. After the streets cooled off a little they were comparing notes on what they heard about the recent riot up in Harlem. The north was becoming as fiery as the south.

Nowhere to run . . . nowhere to hide

August, 1964 dad was getting ready for a gig with Mickey Collins in Chester, PA. The entire house smelled like Right Guard deodorant and Safeguard soap. Mom stayed home with me and watched Friday Night at the Movies. She said a Sidney Poitier movie was coming on that evening. She was in love with Sidney Poitier. She told me he was the epitome of class and poise, a Dr. King of film. A big green window fan kept the living room comfortable. A car honked outside waiting for dad to get a move on. After he left mom gave me a bath and got me ready for bed.

Later that night all hell broke loose. The movie was interrupted. North Philly turned out. From West Philly the sky looked like the sun forgot to set. The porch ladies, Bright Pink, Ms. Doris and High Hips were all piled on Ms. Ruth's porch. Screen doors were slapping as people went back and forth in the house while others were milling up and down the street and the sounds of television, music and police were everywhere. Mom got me up and brought me downstairs and laid me down on the living room sofa in the middle of it all. Nobody saw Johnny Carson that night. I didn't understand what was going on, but felt the tension. The television had live reports about rioting in the street. Mom was jumping up and down all night answering the phone in the kitchen.

Columbia and Ridge Avenues just about burned to the ground. All of America's ugliness came to the surface. The lies were out. Billy clubs were flying. There was a lot of looting going on that night. People broke into store front windows taking clothes, shoes, food or just about anything they could grab a hold of. A few people resorted to pitiful stealing of shoestrings, bobby pins and soap. The telephone rang again and there was a knock at the door. Mom let Ms. Doris in and ran to the phone. I was wide awake by now.

Mama recounted "Your father called that night during an intermission asking if we were okay. He was worried sick. He wasn't sure exactly where the trouble was. All he knew was there were a lot of fires going on. They even stopped the music to make an announcement that all hell was breaking loose around them. They wanted to give people the option to go home or run for cover if they chose, but most chose to keep the party going. He said he'd be home as soon as he could and if it got worse to get out and go up home to Gwynedd. He had rode with Mickey so I had the car."

Burn, baby, burn

Ms. Doris got word that a woman was killed. Mom said she saw people running every which-a-way and it seemed like the entire city was in flames. She said she saw a man on T.V. running down the street with a sofa on his back. Who knows how he pulled it off? Another shot captured a woman and a man carrying a table while children were carrying the chairs going down the street. Ms. Doris and mom were both nearly in shock. They sat down looking at TV and each other. Ms. Ruth hopped the banister crashing in the door talking about her sister. Mama said she heard *Dancing in the Street* over the rambling and it got louder by the second. It was Mr. Willie in the car the porch ladies talked so much about. As big as it was, they called it a short. In one step they all jumped up and headed for the door.

"Lawd it is something out here tonight. I wouldn't be surprised if it came this way!" Mr. Willie said as he turned off the engine and got out of the car like it was about to catch fire. His shirt was soaking wet.

Mom squeaked "Oh sweet Jesus. Please don't talk like that! What in the Sam Hill is going on?!"

Ms. Doris was frantic "I heard some lady was killed!"

Mr. Willie took a hanky from his shirt pocket and began to wipe his brow and said "Hard to say. One thing for sure, there's a lot of blood in the street tonight. These folks out here done gone crazy."

Mom said "What you doing out in this mess Willie?"

"I was coming from my sister's house on Taylor Street. She just had a baby girl. I was getting ready to leave and I heard all this carrying on, but I didn't know where it was coming from. I hauled ass. Cops are everywhere. I tried to cut down Ridge, but I couldn't make it. I didn't see fire, but I smelled smoke and thought to myself, let me get the hell outta here!"

Mom said "What's your sister gonna do with a brand new baby? Why didn't you bring her here with you?!"

Mr. Willie said "She and her old man are alright. They're burning down the stores. Nobody is burning houses. If she stays in the house she'll be okay. I gotta go. I sure needs me a drink tonight." Mr. Willie walked into the darkness toward his home.

The phone rang again. It was Cousin Verlie telling mom to come up to mom's home in Gwynedd, PA. Mom decided to hold tight and wait for dad to come home. I fell asleep sometime later, but mom told me after a while everyone calmed down a little and went home. She sat watching television and waited for dad. He found us both sleeping on the sofa. I awoke to the sound of keys at the door. The television was signing off. I saw the American flag waving in the air to The National Anthem. Everything was alright once he walked through the door. He told mom his story about the fiery night while picking me up to bed. The television had a full screen of salt and pepper. I fell asleep in his arms.

Labor Day weekend was filled with American flags blowing from front porch windows and talk about what the newspapers said about the riot—what the people said—and what might happen next. The Philadelphia Tribune, a black newspaper said black folks were angry from enduring relentless abuse, stores and landlords ripping them off and violent attacks from police covered up in lies. The rioters reportedly had no weapons. They didn't attack homes or government buildings. They attacked businesses they claimed gypped them out of their money. The Daily News, the main stream paper, said hoodlums were running wild in the street. Communist Negroes were attacking cops—gone ape shit. We weren't alone. Cleveland and Chicago were fanning flames. Harlem had just cooled off the month before. College campuses were upset with demonstrations. The Free Speech Movement was taking hold. In the south people and tree bark were blown away by fire hoses. In 1965 Malcolm X was assassinated in February and in August, Watts burned for a few days. A couple of years later Newark, New Jersey and Detroit, Michigan went up. Each revolt seemed to be worse than the last. Then there was a war was going on across the world in a place called Vietnam that nobody seemed to know much about.

My folks and I took a ride out to see the war torn area. The first thing that struck me was the smell—a dark lingering smell that crept from piles of charred wood. Buildings were burned down to the bone. I saw daylight beaming in from what was a ceiling. The sidewalks were covered in a watery tar and glittered with glass. Half burned cars lined the curb. That terrible smell bothered me. The mom and pop shops got it bad. Shapiro's Shoe Store and Nevin's Drug Store were gone. A big doll was hanging half way out of the door wearing a few charred rags and just beyond her head was a surviving street light that just blinked red. Dad turned onto Ridge Avenue. Piggy's and the Checker Club were fine. Bars and homes were untouched. Dad turned off Ridge to Master Street. They stopped at Twenty First Street. They took me to the place where they used to live and introduced me to Mr. Cook. They wanted to check on the widower who wasn't feeling well to see how he survived the nightmare. They talked about his experience that night. He was still quite upset. Peace was hard to find.

As fall rolled around it seemed tensions cooled along with the temperatures. Children were going back to school and the porch ladies disappeared. Autumn wasn't official until dad and I went out to gather leaves with the rest of the neighbors. I loved to jump in a pile of freshly raked leaves. Sometimes I really got on dad's nerve because he had to rake them up again. He plopped me on the porch and closed the gate while he finished. I watched him and the other neighbors set the leaves on fire after sunset. While several piles of fires grew, I munched on a ginger snap cookie and watched the cool crisp air turned blue with smoke carrying the scent of burning leaves. The ashes were swept away and hosed down the sewer hole at the corner the kids insisted on calling the *sewey* hole. Autumn afternoons and evenings were filled with children playing anything they wanted freely without rules. It did not have to be a learning experience, it was just fun. When we fell we spit on the wound and kept playing. If we dropped a piece of candy we kissed it up to God and ate it. Children gave up their seat on the bus to elders without prompting. When we were angry with each other we fought it out and made up later. The police were never called. Then again children never had weapons. If anyone was caught cursing they were spanked by any neighborhood adult who happened to hear, and I never heard adults use profane language towards children.

Sometime during the fall, dad started his own band, The Bennie Lyons Orchestra. He had about eight men who regularly rehearsed at our home to prepare for weekend affairs. Bootsy Barnes, Rufus Harley, Sonny Hockster, Kent Pope, Tony Williams and Sonny Fortune were just a few of the people who began to frequent our house for impromptu jam sessions. They rocked the house with Herbie Hancock's *Watermelon Man* and Bill Doggett's *Honky Tonk*.

I remember the musicians filing in our house carrying their cases. The sax man pulled out his bright shiny saxophone. It was in two pieces. I sat on the living room sofa looking into the empty dining room and watched him put it together. He put a strap around his neck while sucking on his mouthpiece. Meanwhile the drummer, Mr. Jimmy Griffin filed in with several large drums wrapped in plastic covers. He brought a carpet remnant to place on our hardwood floor before he set up. I watched him as he pulled out his toms and snare drum. Then he attached the sock cymbal onto his bass drum. He pulled the cymbals out and mounted them on top of the drum set. I liked the hi-hat. I liked the sound it made. At the same time Ray Carter, the bass man was tuning up and dad was tightening his strings. Another sax man and a trumpet man came into the house. Mr. Carter started doodling with his bass. I think every organ in my body turned to jello, but I liked it. Dad said something to the guys then started counting. Together they made the most beautiful melody. It sounded something like what dad had been playing on the hi-fi all week. I brought that memory up to mom years later. She told me the tune I heard was *Satin Doll*. She said it was a Duke Ellington song composed by Billy Strayhorn and was considered a standard piece. Dad started some of his affairs with that song. I became fascinated with musical notes and captivated by each sound I heard. Sometimes they played only a part of a song, sixteen to thirty two bars over and over again, until it was burned into my brain. It was during this time in my life that I heard how a song was put together. I learned almost every melody and lyric from rock and roll to jazz to blues to rhythm and blues. That's when music became a part of my little soul.

Merry Christmas Baby . . . you sure did treat me right

"Mom, remember when Christmas didn't start until after Thanksgiving? Christmas seemed to have had a different spirit. People didn't just bring presents, but they brought themselves to the tree. Every door was open. Food was everywhere. I felt a lot of love. Remember that mom?"

"You know I do. We didn't have pumpkins and Santa Claus all mixed up together. I used to take you into town on Wednesday. The stores were open until nine o'clock. We strolled up and down for a while taking in the sights. It was a day for us to be together and enjoy the holiday. Market Street was all aglow. I parked at Lits. They had a garage and a car repair in the back. That's where The Enchanted Village was. Oh, how you loved that."

"Oh yea mama! It was like walking back in time to 1700s England at Christmas. They had the blacksmith, the baker and a toy maker. The scene was covered in snow that had the warmest glow. Snowmen and Christmas trees were everywhere. The life-sized puppets came alive! I felt like I walked into another world. I used to look through the little windows at the cozy fireplace and the lady in the kitchen rolling doe and another scene where a family sat at the table ready for dinner. I wanted to jump in! That was Christmas for me. At the end was Santa Claus. I sat on his knee and told him my wish list."

"I still have the pictures. Then we went on to start shopping. I had a store charge for Lits and Gimbels department stores. They were in your father's name. Not even a white women could get credit in her name. I used the card at Christmas and maybe Easter. People didn't have all of these credit cards like now. Black folks could hardly get any credit unless it was a rip-off. Everybody I knew had cash and carry or put it on lay-away."

I remembered watching mom stick a match in the oven floor to light the pilot. Soon the familiar smell of Christmas Eve lit the house. Cinnamon, vanilla and nutmeg mixed with the soft aroma of pine from the tree. I still don't know why I liked the taste of batter better than the cake. I licked the paddles and the bowl while mom carefully placed the cake pan into the oven. She made homemade lemon orange frosting by shredding the peel from each fruit. The house was toasty with Kenny Burrell's *A Soulful Christmas* playing on the Hi-Fi. Our window was wrapped in laurel and glowed with big lights of every color. I sat on the empty dining room floor eating a slice of pie watching dad decorate our three dollar tree coated with a can of snow. And before long someone was ringing the bell. Good wishes poured in the door. Mom had prepared all kinds of food. She had TV trays set up in the living room for her guests. Some people had gifts, others didn't and it didn't matter. They all filled the house with love and laughter. Hundreds of Christmas cards lined the banister and red candles burned softly on the living room table next to a large dish of my favorite clear-color toy candy. Every night we either had company or we went visiting. Christmas Day for me brought Show and Tell, View Master, tea sets and my beautiful white doll babies. Christmas was for children mama said, but New Years was for grown folks. I was almost a teen before I saw the ball drop on Times Square, but I remember New Years Day was filled with The Mummers parade and black eye peas. The house overflowed with people recalling every gathering throughout the holiday. A man had to be the first to enter the house on New Years Day. He was welcomed with a bowl of steaming black eye peas. Both were for good luck. It must have been an old tradition for a lot of people. My dad and other dads in the neighborhood made the rounds to everyone's home to make sure each was annually anointed.

1965

Excitement was in the air. I could hardly sleep. Mom was up all night frying chicken, making potato salad and fresh squeezed lemonade she put in a large gallon thermos that had a little spigot on the side. Dad packed the chaise lounge, chairs and umbrella in the trunk and mom stuffed Coppertone and Solarcaine in the duffle bag with dry towels and a change of clothes. We were on our way to Atlantic City the next day. Not one summer went by without at least a few trips to the beach. Atlantic City was *the* place to go.

Mom and dad had a dusty rose colored 1961 Chrysler Windsor that featured push button gears, a big sofa seat and a rear view mirror that rested on the dashboard. Our car was apart of the family. Mom named her Florence. Dad packed everything in the trunk and away we went. The funk of pigs hit us as soon as we got to the New Jersey state line. Before the Atlantic City Expressway there were only two ways to get to Atlantic City from Philadelphia; either the Black or White Horse Pike. We went through every whistle stop town at no more than forty five miles per hour catching occasional red lights. The Garden State lived up to its name. For miles there was nothing to view but corn and tomatoes in between the small towns. Roadside stands displayed the sweetest juiciest peaches, big red beefsteak tomatoes and silver queen corn. Once in a while I saw farm animals from the road. Mom showed me the difference between Holstein and Guernsey cows. The air smelled different as we inched our way toward the shore. I smelled the ocean tinged with a slight funk from the swampland a few miles out from the beach. We came into Missouri Avenue. A patch of projects were to the right and a large parking lot was to the left. That parking lot was our little camp ground for the day.

Atlantic City beaches were segregated, not by law, but by custom. Chicken Bone Beach was on Missouri Avenue and the boardwalk. There were no signs to mark territory. Negroes were parceled off a little patch known as the Blackberry patch. The boardwalk had the usual pizza and hot dog menu. Kentucky fried chicken and other fast food places did not exist. All that left us with was fried chicken and potato salad. The entire beach was loaded with chicken bones, which is probably how it got its name. Dad carried the chaise, chairs and umbrella. Mom had our lunch cooler and thermos while I struggled with the duffle bag. We walked from Arctic Avenue to the Boardwalk entrance which was about three city blocks. We walked across the boardwalk to the steps that led to the beach. We hopped through the blistering sand and found a spot at the end of a long row of people. Dad set up our big umbrella and opened the chairs and chaise. Mom spread out a large blanket for me. A sea of hands greeted us as we were settling in. I started playing with my sand bucket and shovel right away. Mom made sure dad and I were wiped down with Coppertone. I didn't know anything about segregation or the limitations that were apart of it. I just saw how mom and dad's friends made the beach the best place to be. They were having the time of their life.

"Hey Hazel! Bennie! Come on and join the party!" somebody shouted.

"Hey people! I'll be there in a minute" Mom yelled.

Dad turned around and waved. Many of my parents' beach friends were club members of social organizations that were rising to prominence in the black community. They were sprawled out in their finest beach wear complete with rhinestones and sometimes sequins and the sheer wrap around shawl. Blinding diamonds and state of the art wigs and dos were attached to every head. They always sat near the back of the beach the same way people do who want to be seen in church. Beach bunnies and strut queens never hit the water. They weren't there for that. They sat on that hot beach and profiled all day. The ladies were light to brown skinned, some looked almost white. Ms. Pat had olive white skin and green eyes. She had shoulder length dirty blond hair. She was tall and slender and wore a beautiful black bathing suit. She and the other ladies got seductive looks from all men, black and white. The ugly looks they got from women made it all the better. Most of the ladies were Philadelphia Society and South Jersey elite. They huddled together and dished the dirt. This crowd had the entire back end of Chicken Bone, a.k.a. the blackberry patch, diamond row.

There were several coolers filled with ice, sodas and of course chicken and potato salad. Paper plates and cups were arranged neatly on the table. Salt and pepper, hot sauce and olives were next to plastic utensils and napkins. A chest under the table contained brandy, scotch, wine, and gin. Rolling Rock nips and sodas were buried in a mound of ice.

Otis Redding and James Brown blasted from the radio. Everyone had their radio on the same station, so we had our own stereophonic funk. There was only one black station so it wasn't too hard to find, just go to the end of the dial and be thankful for good reception. Under a row of large umbrellas was a card table set up for pinochle, poker or black jack. A comfortable arrangement of chaise lounges, tables and chairs awaited us. I was welcomed by the crew. They treated me as their own.

I didn't have anybody to play with. Nobody there had children my age. At only four or five years old, I wasn't able to wander alone, but I was surrounded by a lot love and care and did enjoy the sun and sand and watching the sea gulls fighting for food so I didn't miss not having playmates. The spirit behind their laughter and fun satisfied me. I saw dad lying back in the chaise talking with the guys. I stayed close to mom with the ladies. They made plates of food and passed it around to whoever was hungry. Some of the men were enjoying a drink and were getting a card game started.

A mix of characters filled up the gang. They loved to show each other their recent accomplishments. They talked about their diamonds, how many gallons of expensive liquor they had, or the keys to a brand new car. Some were buying houses in white neighborhoods. One fool had the nerve to wear his mink coat on the beach! Just to show off. The ladies strutted like peacocks and the men wore too many gold chains on their bare chest before it was popular. But to me they were people who were successful in life. They didn't seem to have a lot of problems like the porch ladies, but they talked just as much. I heard at least ten conversations going at the same time:

"You think they're really going to the moon? Later for the moon they need to tend to these riots going on here. The country is burning down. These young folks are going crazy! Johnson ain't gonna do nothing. I'm glad I'm too old to go to war. WWII was enough for me. Where in the Sam Hill is Vietnam anyway? Cassius Clay changed his named. What is it now? I don't know . . . something. He did it with Liston didn't he? Dr. King better watch it! They got Malcolm! Ahhh! Don't compare Malcolm with King! The Coverdale's just bought a house on Mount Pleasant Road. Yea, they up with there white the folks. Bill just bought Delores another car. I wish I was his woman. You think his wife knows? What would she care? He bought her a new car too! Are you staying over or down for the day? We're staying at Princess. I saw that movie! Shelley Winters was something wasn't she? Yea, he sent the girl to a blind school. I don't like him. He's too much up with the white folks for me. I like those sandals. Where did you get them? These came from Strawbridge's. Hush your mouth!!"

Under the Boardwalk

Princess was a hotspot on Michigan Avenue and filled with a lot of secret drama. There were rooms for rent upstairs. The beach queens hashed over one of the ladies who didn't make it down on that day, but when she did she stayed at Princess for free because she was going with a bartender. She looked almost white and when she walked into the club looking good and smelling better of course all of the men wanted to talk to her and one part of that was buying her a drink. She didn't drink. A man would buy her drink and when he wasn't looking she passed it back to the bartender, her man, who would sell it all over again. Other times the flunky for the night was encouraged to buy someone else a drink, paying for the same drink twice. Instead of vodka or rum, it sometimes was just a glass of water with a slice of lemon. He was the only one who didn't know the difference. They made a killing. She lived in the Wind Gate apartments and had plenty of fur coats and diamond rings for the ball.

Somebody got their head rubbed at the card table and someone else had to rise and fly. The men's side of the camp had a rendition of the Signifying Monkey going strong that kept everybody screaming for a good half hour. I had the best laugh of the afternoon when Mr. Eddie was enjoying a chicken wing while sitting back on the chaise. He was talking with my dad and holding the wing elbow high with his right hand when a sea gull swooped down at missile speed and grabbed the wing right from Mr. Eddie's hand.

He cussed the bird out as a flock began to chase the bird with the wing. Still fuming, he dug in the cooler for another wing. Only this time he kept it low and ate the entire wing without saying a word.

The men drank in the hot sun all day. They got plenty juiced and never once was there a fight or any ridiculous behavior. The men folks seemed to sleep in shifts. While some were dozed off in the chaise lounge, others headed toward the ocean to cool off. It wasn't long before they all had another Gin and tonic drink and kept the party going. The ladies had a little cocktail and enjoyed their beauty and enjoyed watching others enjoy their beauty as well.

My father stood at a fearless six feet, five inches tall and about two hundred and forty pounds. He took time out from the grown folks talk and walked me down to the water. He plopped me on his shoulder and headed out to deeper water where I could travel out in the safety net of his strength. He turned his back to the wave. I had a ball getting washed with the warm ocean water. He taught me how to body surf with the wave holding me firmly, sometimes painfully tight while I learned how to work with the current. Then he gently lifted me up when big waves came letting me ride with it, but not getting out of his powerful grip. He never turned me loose until I was tall enough for my feet to hit the ocean floor.

Our beach camp was a spectacle. Black people stared as they were passing by. White people stopped and stared. They all acknowledged our presence with smiles, frowns or perplexed eyebrows. Whites could frequent our end of the beach much more easily than we could theirs. They tried to appear as if they were just looking around at a safe distance taking it all in. Then they went on their way. Mom said she saw the same people who happened to have passed by earlier. They again had to stop and look, sometimes with a smile and maybe even bopping their head with the music, only this time they may have had someone new with them. I was playing in the sand minding my own business, but I paid attention and heard the grown people talk about it.

Ms. Pat leaned over to mom and said "Hey Hazel, here he comes again. That same man has been back and forth all afternoon, looking at me like he wanna say something. I'm gonna get him for reckless eyeballing with attempt to see!"

Then mom turned around and said "Well he needs to get further and smell better. If we went up on their end sniffing around it'd be a different story. He damn sure wouldn't be tryin to say hi then. Don't pay these people any mind Pat."

Ms. Pat turned at looked again and replied "I've seen him before. I was walking on the boardwalk. He made a pass at me. He said he'd give me fifty dollars to smell my drawers! Girl you know I could have slapped him simple."

Mama said "Humph. It shoulda been me. I'd have something for him."

"Oh, Hazel go on now! These nasty assed men don't mean anybody a bit of good" said Ms. Pat.

I couldn't tell if the stares were with contempt or desire. It's something about those blue and gray eyes that made black folks angry or defensive. It didn't seem to faze my dad. I saw him turn around once in a while. He stared a man down into the ground. My dad was like that. Then he'd turn back like nothing ever happened. I also saw how the soul of black folks could take a seemingly bad situation and turn it into a good time. They certainly had their own fun and a history of experience. I didn't know it at the time, but I was witnessing first hand what soulful meant. It was a pleasurable time simply because the people that were there sincerely cared for, and cherished the company of one another. It wasn't the food, the music or the beach. It was their laughter and liberating spirit that gave me a satisfying feeling deep inside.

My eye was soon tuned in on the activity. It was only then I began to notice what the ladies were talking about. I'd see white folks sneaking over to our spot, or at least taking second looks. Then I felt that familiar tension. There wasn't ever one word spoken. I saw how my parents' friends just gave them a cold icy shoulder, at times enjoying it and then talked about them later. Mom took another look back to the boardwalk. Then she looked at Ms. Pat and said "They don't want us on their part of the beach and then they got the nerve to come snooping over here. They need to go on their goddamn merry way! They could take their shit and shove it because we got ours. Get me another piece of chicken baby."

And they really did. They laughed, danced, drank, joked and just partied their ass off. I heard a sigh of relief in their laughter. They were classy Negroes. Black was still a fighting word. The gang started breaking up around 6pm. The sting of the sun was dying. The beach was clearing out and the boardwalk became more crowded. It was time to get the evening started. African Americans were not welcome to stay at any of the beachfront hotels such as the Tray More, Dennis, Shelburne or Haddon Hall. It wasn't obvious; there were no signs on the door. I can't say black people didn't stay there. If they did, we didn't know them. It was a quiet Jim Crow using the almighty dollar for auxiliary power. It was said that people were turned away with the likely response "sorry we're all filled up." Black folks had to go to the back of town to the rooming houses on Arctic Avenue or Michigan Avenue. Once in a while my parents and I stayed at a place where the one and only bathroom was in a long hallway and mom had to keep an eye out to make a run for it to wash up or just to pee. The room itself was just a large room with two beds, one on opposite sides of the room and it sometimes had a sink. My bed was closest to the window and the green neon light flashed in my face all night long. It was the Waters Rooming House. There was no television, no telephone or air conditioning and definitely no room service.

When we were just down the shore for the day, we changed clothes in the back seat of the car. I was washed with the cold water that was ice cubes at the start of the day. My hair was brushed hard to get out as much sand as possible. We changed and freshened up as best we could and started out to enjoy the evening. We took the jitney near Arkansas Avenue all the way to the northward end of the boardwalk to dine at either Captain Starn's or Hackney's. Captain Starnes was a large docked ship turned into a seafood restaurant. It always had an incredibly long line. It seemed as though it reached back to Philly. When we were seated we were greeted with menus and a photographer to take our picture and make a matchbook cover with it.

After dinner we walked from the beginning of the boardwalk from Captain Starn's down to the main attractions. The water kicked up at high tide and splashed underneath and on top of the boardwalk. It was like walking in the middle of the ocean near the inlet. The sun was gone and the cool ocean breeze was delightful. I was mesmerized by the power of the ocean. I watched the big waves over and again. It was frightening and beautiful. I loved to watch the wave's crash and foam giving no mercy to whatever may be in the line of collision.

The Million Dollar Pier was in its incandescent splendor. I heard joyful screams from the roller coaster clashing with the ocean's roar. The salt air was sultry and filled with mouthwatering aromas of cotton candy, roasted peanuts and popcorn. Dad bought a few tickets at the booth on the pier and took me in hand to enjoy some of the rides. I went on the Tea Cup and boat ride by myself. Dad rode the Ferris wheel and Merry-go-round with me. When he became too tired he asked a parent's permission to offer a free ride to their child to go along with me. I made friends quickly and had a ball.

Mom and dad couldn't do the clubs like they wanted to because they were stuck with me. The beach gang was in their evening glory and mom especially wanted a little bit of it. We strolled back to Kentucky Avenue between Atlantic and Arctic Avenues where the whole street was going on. Since the forties, this was the best place in the world for African American people. Most of the places had resident entertainment and tons of food. It was the most incredible block party I had ever seen.

Libby Spencer's Club Harlem had a line going out of the door and around the corner. From what I remember, the bar was a horseshoe around the stage. Bobby Blue Bland was the feature that night. A beautiful dancer, Ms. Hortense a.k.a. Big Legs had the stage by herself and gave it all she had. I could see from the street how breathtaking she was. She performed in New York before coming to the Delaware Valley.

Wild Bill Davis and Johnny Hodges were a little ways down at Gracie's lil Belmont. Legend had it that Sammy Davis Junior's mother was the bartender there. Wild Bill stomped on the bass organ keys and sent the Negroes crazy. It was pure power. I enjoyed it better than the rides.

The Wonder Garden had Damita Jo, Libistro featured Della Reese and Count Basie. The air was filled with ribs, chicken, seafood and liquor. Music from every club door poured into the street. There was so much good stuff going on people hardly knew which way to go. It was little Harlem. It was all ours. No need to pretend, one could just be. Everyone was looking good and welcoming all who came. Big people looked down at me with a smile and sometimes a bag of potato chips. Lights were dancing from every direction and so was I. The street stayed packed. You could hardly get a car through all the traffic. It was best to park somewhere and walk. The 500 Club was over on Missouri and was mostly white. The Rat Pack appeared there often, but Kentucky Avenue was nothing but a party.

Pick'em and put'em down

Sometime after our Chicken Bone Beach vacation, my parents prepared to go down south. Every year my parents went to Durham, North Carolina to visit my father's family. Mom would be up all night long again frying chicken and making potato salad. Dad put our suitcases in the trunk the night before we left. The next morning we jumped into our beloved Florence. Dad and mom pushed back in unison to adjust the sofa seat to accommodate his extra long legs. We usually went to Delaware to get I-95, but the year after the Chesapeake Bay Bridge was completed we took Route 13 south to see the bridge and tunnel that spanned about twenty miles. The trade winds from the bay spared us the sweltering heat as we journeyed along the stretch of ribbon highway on the deep blue bay. Mom told me stories from her past Route one trips to the south. I gazed out the window, occasionally waving at hitchhikers along the road. Virginia was the longest part of the ride. Mom and dad enjoyed a good laugh when we passed by Po White Highway and Turkey Egg Road. We had to make it to Durham before dark. Dad pulled over at a Phillips 66 gas station somewhere in Virginia to fill up while mom took me behind the station toward the woods to pee. When we returned, it was dad's turn. Mom had these new towelettes called "Wash n Dry" for us to clean our hands and then we had our picnic inside of the car.

We took I-64 to Route 55. Somewhere below the mystical Mason-Dixon Line, time did not change to daylight savings. Mom and dad changed their watches back to standard time. Mom took the wheel over in Dinwiddie. Dad climbed in the back to rest and I sat in front with mom. Mom said in those days the speed limit was seventy miles per hour, so she felt free to put her foot inside of the gas tank. It was getting on toward evening. Two naps later we finally made it the North Carolina state line. A sign read Henderson, 10 miles. We went over the Tar River to Oxford and half way through my third nap, Florence got us to Grandmom Ethel's driveway in Durham.

Grandmom Ethel lived on Enterprise Street, a dusty road filled with clapboard houses and Jackson's store at the corner. Mom always said Grandmom had a run through house. I could run from the front porch right out to the back yard and nothing would stop me. Mom and dad had second thoughts about leaving the house after dark with Pennsylvania tags on their car. Dad backed the car into the driveway so the PA plates were hidden from the road. My aunts and uncles were there to greet us. Grandmom Ethel was a big fluffy woman, the kind that gives those soft, suffocating hugs. After we settled in, I had to take a bath to get ready for bed. Grandmom brought out a giant tin tub and placed it in the middle of the kitchen floor and filled it with hot water from an old black ugly stove. I looked forward to my baths until then. Mom already had a firm hold on me as she took my clothes off to make sure I didn't get away. There wasn't a door or anything to keep other people from parading back and forth. Nobody really paid attention to me, but I felt awkward being the only one in the house with no clothes on. Mom scrubbed me down quickly and wrapped me in a towel and put me to bed. The bed was right next to the front porch window. I fluffed my pillows so I could lay back and see everything happening on the porch through the sheer curtains. It was a hot night with a cool breeze. I listened to every word until I fell asleep. Mom, dad, grandmom Ethel and a couple of my aunts and uncles rocked the night away smacking mosquitoes and wiping sweat as they talked about the Civil Rights Movement. My father's family didn't vote. They didn't like it at all. They didn't think it was worth the effort—or the risk.

Uncle Wesley puffed on a Lucky Strike while talking to dad "That's a chance for them to make a fool of yuh. They might ask you to read the constitution or yuh gotta take some test or count jelly beans. They wanna know your mama's name and what she died with, and then they got this tax you gotta pay. Why should I pay to vote somebody into office who wouldn't like nothing better than to see me hanging from a tree?"

Uncle Wesley was tall just like dad. He had the same ruddy skin, only Uncle Wesley had hazel eyes. Uncle Leroy poured another little taste of corn liquor into his favorite jelly jar. He was a dumpy brown skinned man with a fat cabbage head, but was the sweetest man in his heart. He stuttered sometimes when he talked and wasn't always easy to understand. He took a swig then said "Dock, doc, Dockta Kang come down her startin all dat trouble, getting white folks upset. I don't know how he thank he gone change dese white folks down her, ain't lack up yonda, yawl vote and go places and even talk back to white folks."

Uncle Wesley rocked his chair hard and said "I wish he'd go back to Lanta and take all dat noise wit'em." Uncle Wesley spit a piece of tobacco in the air. "Looka her, I want the same thang everybody wants, but I ain't tryin to do colored time in Charlie's jailhouse see? Ain't none a this gonna make any difference anyway. Dey still be hatin."

Dad was sitting near the end of the porch sipping on Knee-Hi orange soda and responded by saying "Yea, I can't say I blame you for that. It seemed like all of this trouble just started out of nowhere. But we got find a way to deal with it. They carrying on up the road too. It ain't just down here. I just don't want to see anybody get hurt."

As they talked I learned that they called white men "Mr. Charlie" and white folks in general they called "gray". Black folks were called blue. White women were called "Ms. Lynch" unless you worked for one, then she was Ms. Ann. I heard the porch ladies say something like that too.

"Look, Johnson got the voting bill last year. You can eat in town at the lunch counter and ride the bus now. Just yesterday you couldn't do that. Dr. King helped to bring all of that on yuh know" Mom said. She loved Dr. King.

Uncle Wesley flashed his hazel eyes at mom "And you thank I'm gonna eat what dem white folks made back in dat kitchen? How I know dey won't spit in it or somethin? I'm smart enough not to eat after people who are filled with hate. He gonna get us killed by upsettin white folks and having coloreds scared to death. What yuh thank gonna happen tuh us after he gone? We all in trouble! They runs up on yuh anytam. Can't go to town to sign up—they know where yuh live! I don't want nuttin to do with it. Dem white kids come down her tryin to get folks to sign up. Nawsir! We got folks missin now and don't know where dey at, but we know what happened to'em. Mista Myers was on his way back to Durham from Rocky Mount. Never did see'em no moe. Found his car. He was wit da NAACP. No funeral, no investigation—nothing. About five years ago now."

Uncle Wesley was a proud man just like dad, but he was scared of white folks in the way anyone would be afraid of a rabid dog. Mama shook her head in disbelief. I thought about what Ms. Ruth said on the porch that day. She said white folks go out at night down south. And that they wear sheets and hunt down Negroes to kill. I remembered that as I sat up in bed looking out the window across the road into a black southern night. Suddenly the bedroom had dark corners I hadn't noticed before. The blackness of the woods across the street was suddenly threatening. The back of Uncle Leroy's head was right at my window. He said "It's a good way to loose yuh job and get yuh house boined down. Dat dere voting is white folks business, not ours. Dat's just the way it is." Uncle Leroy was somewhere between talking and preaching while nodding his head left to right. "I goes to work, go to the Chicken Coop and get me a little drank and go home and get in tuh bed." Grandmom never said a word.

My Uncle Jimmy was known as Buttercup. He lived in D.C. and loved to party. I heard his feet clomp up the plank steps onto the front porch. He stopped by midway into the conversation and totally changed the subject "Hey Benny Lee! How yuh doing? What time you get into town?" Buttercup said as he kissed my mom.

"We pulled up a few hours ago. We're just resting up from the road" said Benny Lee.

"Come' on. Let's go to the Stallion Club tonight. Otis Redding is supposed to be there" Buttercup said.

"I remember the Stallion Club. Oh, I love me some Otis, come on Benny, let's go. Your mother will take care of Terri" said Mama. "Naw, you go ahead. I'm gonna get some sleep" Dad replied.

"Well, I'm heading home. See yuh tomorrow Benny Lee" Uncle Leroy chimed in.

Dad wasn't too concerned because he knew the club was on the colored end of town and they didn't have to take the highway to get there. I heard the clop-clop of feet walking off from the porch onto the front yard and then the car started. I knew Florence's motor anywhere. Grandmom came into where I was lying in bed wide awake and coddled me for a little while. Dad came in soon after and kissed me goodnight. Grandmom left and dad slipped into the bed on the other side of the room.

"Gimme the keys Hazel. Let me drive. Hold on Leroy, I'll take you home" said Uncle Buttercup.

Mom told me years later about the night she went out with Uncle Jimmy and Aunt Francis. North Carolina was a dry state. They could have drinks in a glass, but the bottle had to be kept under the table. It never did make sense to her, but that's the way it was. She told me Otis tore the place up with his song *My Girl*. It had just come out. Mom said she did the Cha-cha with my uncle when Otis did *Stand by Me*.

The next day dad backed out our car and took me and my uncle Wesley for a ride through town. He took me to several different homes to see people he said were my cousins. Warmth and welcome were apparent anywhere we went. The first thing everyone wanted to do was offer food, but thankfully dad said we couldn't stay long. We had to get to Kroger's to do grocery shopping for grandmom. I was happy to tag along with dad. I was desperate to have something to do. I missed being home. I grew tired of the few toys I had. Neither mom nor dad read to me before bedtime. Grandmom Ethel didn't have a television and there wasn't any music. I wasn't allowed to go any further than the front porch. I wasn't allowed in the back at all because there were snakes in the woodpile. The afternoons were long, hot and terribly silent. I played with a cat that lived under the porch and slept most afternoons away to escape the boredom. What a difference experience it was with people in the south. They weren't always in such a hurry. They didn't seem to be as angry or belligerent as the ones I heard about in Philly. I was used to people getting cussed out in their face and maybe an ass whipping too. No wonder my uncles didn't like northerners coming down the road. To them, northern people were trouble. Mama always said she couldn't live down south. She didn't possess a compliant soul and would soon be in trouble. We never stayed very long. On our way home I looked at the rivers and trees with different eyes. The peaceful thicket that is so gently loved by the rain and beautifully radiant in the sun didn't appear so peaceful to me now. I had horror stories in my memory of the beatings and lynchings. The lush forests hid the blood and muffled the cries of people who looked just like me. The trees seemed to harbor evil and its silhouette in the nighttime sky intensified the threat that lurked in my mind.

Tell your mama, tell your pa, we gonna integrate Arkansas . . .

It was just as hot in Philly as it was in Durham. Before mom unpacked our suitcase the news was reporting a riot had broken out in Watts. It looked worse than the one in Philly some years before. Mama said more people were dying and the country was going to burn into hell for sure. She remembered almost every time she turned the television on another city was up in flames. Philly was having rallies and protests. Sometimes famous people from out of town came to speak to a gathering of people about "The Movement". A local organization called Citizens for Progress which was headed by Novella Williams sponsored some of these gatherings. Ms. Novella was a brilliant speaker. She introduced an agenda for black people that included knowing their rights, how to advocate for themselves and ways to act upon it. She believed that police brutality and poverty should be addressed. Luncheons featured so called rabble rousing notables like Jesse Jackson and Stokely Carmichael. Organizations were becoming prominent in the Philadelphia area. Some were social groups that sponsored affairs and gave scholarships to underprivileged children. Others focused on the political agenda and the plight of poor and underclass black people who were completely ignored. My parents had the privilege of preparing for one of the affairs. The Bennie Lyons Band played at the Sheraton Hotel affair, on Kennedy Boulevard in Philadelphia. It was the first time they performed in a major ballroom.

Mama said guests were seated eight to a table. They feasted on baked chicken and rice with string beans almandine. Black intelligentsia hosted affairs speaking on behalf of all voiceless Negroes who were tired of being afraid and tired of feeling ashamed. Negroes were tired of what democracy had offered them so far. They were tired of their humanity being violated by the status quo and they were enraged by the lies that hid injustice.

They spoke of how blacks were systematically disenfranchised with being denied jobs and decent housing. The dilemma was sure to continue because too many city schools had inferior curriculums and facilities. The common consensus was that Nationalism would be the only way to overcome these obstacles. The plea was to create and maintain a black economy and educate our children. It meant getting dope and crime out of our neighborhoods. We, as Afro-Americans would have to have unity of thought as well as unity of action. Many believed that an example must be set for young children not to depend on the white man to take care of us; instead, we must learn to take care of ourselves.

There was a need to become not only politically aware, but to gain political power and to vehemently challenge contradictions and to internalize a nationalist agenda by building a black economic system. Citizens for Progress challenged the audiences to own real estate, to have more control in schools and to nurture their families. Negroes had to acquire a statehood to free themselves from slanted perceptions and calculated conclusions imposed on them by the dominant culture. Progress was being made. Leon Sullivan launched OIC and Julian Bond became a congressman. A piece of paper said that civil rights for everyone was the law of the land and another piece of paper stated everybody had the right to vote.

Light, Bright and damn near white

African Americans had a war of their own going on during that time. Negroes were trying to make up their mind about class and identity. Skin complexion and hair texture were pulling people apart. In an attempt to overcome and rise above the degradation, black people no longer identified with the term "Coloreds" and defined themselves as "Negroes" and as a result moved away from niggers and became neighbors with blacks. Upwardly mobile blacks were often met with hostility for not being black enough, but for being bourgeoisie, while those left behind were accused of being too black or gutbucket negroes. I saw it. People rolled their eyes, signified or avoided certain people altogether that they didn't even know! They thought they knew what others thought or were about by the way they looked or where they lived. Jealousy and contempt for one another kept the air thick with distrust. Light skin carried social weight which black folks seemed to despise, but also adored, especially as it pertained to females. If good hair accompanied light skin, an air of privilege and envy followed her. Her womanhood was of a more precious flavor. My mother, a brown skinned woman, took special note of how people were treated differently sometimes because of their complexion. I never noticed my sandy brown hair or light complexion, mostly because mom never brought it to my attention. She never used it as a status or a weapon as to who I should play with.

Mom told me "Back then color and hair were everything. There were more bleaching creams and beauty treatments to make black skin light; for instance, Mr. Palmer, bleach and glow. Women used make-up three shades too light and washed their face with lemon juice. Women used anything! I've met people who were proud to sling their hair and say their grandfather was a white man. They had the prettiest children who could do no wrong. They were little doll babies everybody slobbered over because they were light and some had the hair to go along with it. Some people didn't have their children playing with or being friends with dark children. I showed you pictures from parties' long ago and there was not one chocolate bunny in the crowd. See, it was two fold. The light brights got in good with white folks—they were more acceptable. Then they made it into middle class. They worked their ass off like anybody else, but once they had the houses and cars that most black folks didn't have, they turned their ass completely wrong side. Everybody wasn't like that, but too many of them were. They couldn't eat fried chicken anymore, stopped listening to James Brown and sat around the house all dressed up and going nowhere. Just to make sure you knew they arrived, some would "happen" to have a Nan Duskin or Bonwitt Teller shopping bag sitting in the corner. Men folks, especially dark men would do anything to get a high yella woman. He'd eat forty yards of her shit and would have two jobs so he could buy her diamond rings and mink stoles to keep her—and he got her too. She could have any man she wanted—and she did. Light skinned men with pretty eyes, those Smokey Robinson type men with nice hair could have any woman he wanted—and he did. See where it's going? It was the underground war. As if it wasn't enough dealing with white folks and their shit, you had to be snubbed by your own people. High yella heifers or black bitches—take your pick. It's a hell nobody ever dared to put on the table. That's why I told you whites aren't necessarily your enemy and blacks ain't necessarily your friend. Some things aren't black or white, it's just people. Watch who you love and never hate."

Mom told me that all the time. I wasn't even ten years old yet. I didn't know how to figure it out. I was torn between black and white, light-skin, dark-skin, and the neighborhood versus the residence. I didn't know exactly what pride was that I heard so much about. What was shame? Mom told me what her grandmother used to tell her. She told me to never bow my head to anybody. It doesn't matter if they're black or white or half white. They still have to wash their behind just like everybody else.

She said "I wished you had known your great-grandmother. She used to tell me about how people are. That their mouth ain't no prayer book and their ass ain't no bible. You take up after what people say and you will be one confused mess. Some people who tried to be so way out were some of the most deceitful people I ever met.

Many of them were not as bright as they wanted you to think they were. Listen to your heart and mind. Be true to yourself because you're the only one who has to go to bed and get up with it. Always hold your head high and never apologize for who you are; maybe for something you said or did and think about that twice, but never for who you are. Either way, you'll make friends or you'll make enemies, so you might as well be who you are."

Moving forward didn't relieve stigmas. Progress in black hands somehow lost some value. People were labeled as being uppity. Some called them smart niggers. Black folk's progress seemed to be nothing more than white folk's leftovers. Their old neighborhoods were our new ones. Mama told me when only white folks had Cadillac cars, all coloreds could do was wish. When enough coloreds could afford them, it was called a nigger car. In spite of our troubles we could still have good time on Saturday night, our only night of relief, affectionately known as nigger night. Those who managed to save a little money and live a little better were nigger rich. When black women were able to finally get fur coats it was a problem with animal rights people. She was a part of and a witness to the frenzy to move up and create social distance between those who had and those who didn't. She shook her head remembering how people tried to be the toast of the town.

"This middle class thing exploded sometime after *the war*. There had always been a middle class, but by the early sixties it grew. The factories and defense plants were going strong. More black people owned their own businesses. It was the first time many black women had a job outside of the white folk's kitchen. People who were doing well had televisions, a telephone, a washing machine and a nice car. A lot of people didn't have those things. It took off by the early sixties. They weren't all bourgeoisie people with a big education and jobs. Most of them worked in factories. People worked and saved their money. We didn't waste up stuff like today. Nothing was made to use just once and throw away. We used cloth diapers and glass bottles. We used mayonnaise jars, cookie jars or whatever it took to save money. I opened a savings account with ten dollars. A year later I had about five or six hundred dollars. You could buy a car with that kind of money. Of course people got six percent interest that wasn't taxed. We didn't have taxes, fees and surcharges to steal it away. You could make a nickel with a soda bottle. That's how most people did it. That's how they bought their home and some began to send themselves and their children to college. Later people started getting the good jobs. The doors were beginning to open; The Navy Yard, Quartermaster, Signa Core and the Frankford Arsenal. That put us on mortgage row. Black folks created a world of prestige of their own.

I listened to her go on about how black folks, especially people we knew, worked and strived to make a better life. Some working class people saved their way into middle class. Mama said it was because of the Depression. Going through that time made people save everything they had. She said some people were finally able to get checking accounts and wanted everybody to know they had one. They would leave their checkbook sitting on the dining room table or someplace where anybody could glance upon it.

I laughed and said to mom, "Ain't that something? People had to learn how to write a check and fill out deposit and withdrawal slips. And now having a check book is slowly fading. People pay bills with automatic withdrawals and PayPal accounts! Banks counted coins for free. Now the banks charge you to count your coins. You know I have to wrap coins now before the bank will accept them. I remember my first savings account passbook. You took me to PSFS in Cheltenham and opened a saving account for me starting with my penny jar. It amounted to twenty dollars. Every time I got something for my birthday or Christmas, I made a deposit. By the time I was twelve, I had about three hundred dollars. Just think about the money I had on interest alone. It made me want to save even more. I still have a big jar of change."

Mom replied "Six percent straight up. No taxes, no fees, nothing to steal it away from you. That helped. People were able to save. I had to introduce you to how money worked. Every time somebody gave you a quarter I didn't want you running to the store to buy candy. Spend a nickel, but save the twenty cents. Otherwise you'll be broke the rest of your life. That's what kept too many black people broke. They spent every dime they had trying to impress others and prove that they were more than what they were. The best way is to save your money and fix up what you have. I know people who did that and they had comfortable homes and didn't have to starve to do it. It all started by saving money. That was pride because it represented the fruits of hard work and sacrifice."

As black people began to get better jobs and buy homes and cars, they also began to acquire different lifestyles and taste. Their pride was reflected in a change in décor, fashion, cuisine, behavior and beliefs. These changes were completely foreign to most black people and used as an indication of who was or wasn't ready for admittance into the middle class. For some it was the very first time the dispossessed had the power to live a better life and to make a choice. They had a different outlook on life. But as people prospered something changed. Negroes collapsed into different yet expanding groups who didn't speak to one another or listen with the same voice and they began to disconnect themselves from other people. A strange coldness fell on some relationships. Negroes who acquired property and good paying jobs began to distance themselves from those who had less and considered them low class. Smugness filled the air. The porch ladies investigated. Gossip became more vicious. I teetered on the fence and was a witness of frustration and utopia as a little girl. Mom and dad wanted to have more and to be a part of the expanding middle class. Mom liked to socialize with people but she didn't like raunchy carryings on. She liked the cosmopolitan taste of life, but she didn't like the stuck-up attitudes of some of the in-crowd either. Mom liked to help people, but didn't like people leaning on her. She saw herself going back and forth trying to find a balance of holding on to herself and flexing with the company she kept. I asked her about the changing social structure of that time. Mama reflected on the memories of her young and vibrant life with an autumn mind.

"Well, you know when some people get up on their feet they act like they don't know you anymore. High and mighty we called it. That got people more than anything.

Some of them acted like they were born into money and never knew hard times. On the other end, when you get up on your feet, you have to cut some people loose because they will drag you down. They'll get in the way of your progress. They'll beg and borrow from you to death. If some figure you to have more than they do, then to them you can afford it and they don't see anything wrong with it. That got people too. I had to cut some people loose. Every time I turned around somebody wanted to borrow an onion, borrow a cup of milk, they needed fifty cents or a slice of bread. If you didn't give it to them they got mad and started talking you down because to them you think you're better. A lot of fights started like that. People began to avoid one another. I got tired of it. There was a time I was on my ass too, but I worked to get out of it and in the mean time I did without. I thought the Depression taught everybody about that."

"But mama, didn't you tell me that borrowing from one another was just about the only way many black families survived? When nobody wanted to hire black people, when black men couldn't take care of their families or they were surviving on starvation wages, and when they first came north and had nowhere to go that neighbors and relatives had to depend on each other to get through it?" I inquired.

She said "That's right they did. But that was to help each other to struggle in their own right. Nobody sat on their behind. If I take somebody in my home I expect them to look for work, go to school and help with house chores. When they're able to stand on their own they pay me back by doing well for themselves. That's what helping somebody means. I'll take care of your children if you are looking for a job or have errands to run, but don't get lost. But some people will move up with you and get comfortable and expect you to take care of them. Every time they needed something they had their hand out looking for somebody to give it to them, rather than getting up and getting it for themselves. That's where the trouble began. That's where some black folks started falling apart. People who were getting along in life didn't appreciate having their pockets picked. Others who were still having a hard time were quick to call them snooty, uppity, got brand new. It's always a catch twenty two when it comes to pulling yourself up and out of a situation or lifestyle you have outgrown."

I responded with "I know what you mean mama. Anytime somebody has to go along to get along, they're usually going along with nothingness and getting along with stagnation. To grow in any capacity almost always means there is going to be fight of some sort. It didn't stop the parties though did it?"

"Damn sure didn't" She replied.

Having a Party!

House parties were the highlight of most weekends. I remember when mom and dad were having theirs. She didn't invite any of the porch ladies, only her friends. Mom would be up the night before getting the cultural cuisine together. Dad hand picked the records he wanted to play and stacked them inside the hi-fi. I couldn't wait until I was old enough to get dressed up and have the same kind of fun as mom and dad. Mom loved to entertain and have a good time. She had the house ready. She put out the good towels and guest soap in the bathroom, washed off the TV trays and spread out her best tablecloth and set the table. Then she went upstairs to bathe and dress. After a dab of Evening in Paris perfume, she was hostess ready. Mom called Michelle, Ms. Barbara's daughter from up the street to baby-sit me. I was ready for bed when she arrived, but would have rather peeked through the stair spokes than stay upstairs and watch television. Mom and dad's guests arrived dressed in suit and tie and the ladies were in cocktail dresses. When they began to dance, I watched their feet. I caught their fever. They hollered and danced, laughed and ate. My insides were exhilarated.

Let's Go Get Stoned

Mom recalled "In the early days it was fine. Motown was just coming out. Aretha was new. We enjoyed each other. There weren't rules and restrictions. We had party records we used to play. They were comedy records like Moms Mabely and Redd Foxx. I still have the record by a duo named Cornbread and Biscuits. The record was called *Last of the Big Time Spenders*. We would sit and listen and laugh our behinds off! Later we got the party rocking. We did dances called the Madison and the Continental all night long. It was just like the Soul Train line. Men were on one side and women were on the other side. They came down the line doing the Continental. You spelled the name with your feet as you danced, see? You had to make the C and turn around on the O and dip it down on the N. Then you crossed the T! We had a ball with that dance. We bopped and slopped until dawn. I used to love a record by the Philip Upchurch Combo called *You Can't Sit Down* and Bill Doggett came out with *Honky Tonk*. Ramsey Lewis had a record called *The In-Crowd*. When the needle hit that record, it was something else! My friend Elsie could do the Philly Slop. It looked like she took her behind and threw it on her back! While she was grinding out the floor, I grabbed a napkin and fanned her behind—she was hot! Everybody was trying to outdo the other person. Sometimes we had amateur hour. We sang and danced for each other. It was so much fun. If the party went on long enough, I started fixing breakfast. But you know there's always one. Occasionally parties invited smiling enemies in the house. Sometimes everybody knew what was going on but the host. Stuff around the house came up missing. I've gone to some parties where the house was absolutely beautiful and didn't somebody pick it apart? They talked about the host, stole the ashtray, or complained about the food. After a while, it stopped a lot of house parties. There were a lot of two faced bitches smiling and lying. They will stab you in the back then come to your house with a smile, eat up your food and drink your liquor and burn a cigarette hole in your sofa and call it an accident."

"Remember when you told me about a party you went to with some friends of friends? One of the ladies got pissed with the hostess. It was in West Philly somewhere wasn't it?" Mom had told me so much; I was beginning to get my stories mixed up.

"Oh yeah, that wasn't West Philly. The party was in Sharon Hill. These women were neighbors and friends in West Philly, but Dolly and her husband bought a house in Sharon Hill. It was beautiful too. They had a Cadillac parked on the car port and a nice back yard. The old neighbor was invited to the party and was she ever jealous. It turned out that the neighbor went to use the bathroom and she took the toothbrushes and swirled them in the toilet bowl. Ain't that something? See, that's what some bitches will do" she recalled.

"But mom, how on earth did you ever know that happened? No way she did it and then turned around and talked about it. If she did, she's nasty and stupid" I said.

"Bitches talk too" she answered.

"I'll be damned" I responded.

Shake and Finger Pop

Mom and dad went to cabarets sometimes as guests and other times as musicians. They were in the early days of their entertainment business and meeting new and different people all of the time. Mom said cabarets were inside picnics. There was only live music on stage and some cabarets had two bands. It was the talk of the week before the dance and if something happened, it was the talk of the week after the dance. Ballrooms and dance halls were all over the city and were the only places black people were allowed to have dances. Major hotel ballrooms were not available to people of color.

I brought out an old photo album and went through it with mom. Although I was just a little girl, I often felt like I was as much apart of that time as she was. Mom hadn't seen the pictures in years. Most of the people in them have passed on. Mom took me back to more than forty years of what it was like to be young and vibrant in the world of 1965.

She said "My friends and I had such a good time. Your father and I would get ready for one of these dances. I had Barbara's daughter from up the street to watch you. We picked up my friend Lillian on the way to the Imperial ballroom. We were dressed up something beautiful. Our hair and make-up were gorgeous. Lillian used to love to see me do a dance called the Mashed Potatoes. James Brown had come out with the record, Mashed Potatoes U.S.A. I used to love to see her Bop on the floor. She could sling those hips some kinda way. We drank all night long and nobody got out of hand. When the dance was over I brought a carload of folks back to the house and fixed breakfast. The ladies went in the kitchen and got the sausage and grits going while the men sat in the living room cracking up laughing and having a good time. Those were the Saturday nights we had. The night I really started singing was in Chester, PA."

"Now mama, you know you got to tell me how that happened. What was the name of the place?"

She replied "I don't remember. I know it was at 6th and Edgemont. Your father had his own band by then. He had a singer, Marion. She was good, but I knew I could have done better. My friend Estelle and some other ladies were with me. We were on the floor partying and table hopping. Every table had something to drink, so by intermission everybody was a little tuned up. After intermission I told your dad I wanted to sing a song."

"What did dad say?" I asked.

"He said no at first. But I kept on him. Come on Benny I said, let me do *The More I See You*. We hadn't rehearsed it or anything. I didn't even know my key so I hummed a little in his ear. That was all he needed. He finally said alright, alright. Then he turned to the band and said 'Fellas, The More I See You.' The intro started. I grabbed that microphone and that was it. I tore that song up!" She said.

"And it started just like that?" I wanted to know.

"What did I tell you? I just fell right into it. I had to do that song two or three times. Estelle was out there on the floor. She hollered to go on Hazel! Get it Girl!" she said.

I sang to mom "My arms won't free you, and my heart won't try!"

"I had it gone that night. That was the end of Marion. From that time on it was Benny Lyons Orchestra featuring vocals by Hazel" she replied.

"You know it didn't matter that some places were off limits to black people did it?"

"No indeed. We cut the rug. Philly was hot. During the sixties there were well established clubs and dance halls all over the place. Your father and I hit just about all of them. In North Philly we had the Blue Note. I saw Billie Holiday there when I first came to Philly."

"Where was that mom?" I inquired.

"It was at 16th and Ridge. Then we went to Butler's Paradise at 21st and Jefferson. Café Society was on Columbia Avenue around Eighth or Ninth Street. Zanzibar was big and then there was the Tropical Garden at 19th and Oxford. It was considered shameful to stay home on Saturday night. There was too much going on. It was all live music and some places had nice dance floors" she remembered.

"That was all in North Philly, huh? Did those places have cabarets?" I asked.

"Cabarets were mostly at ballrooms like the Venango and, let me see now, oh The Blue Horizon" she said.

"What about when you moved to West Philly? Where did you go then?" I asked.

"Your father and I still went to North Philly here and there. The West Philly places were mostly on the main strips; 52nd Street and 60th Street. We had the 421 Club and the 366; the Coup Deville and the Round Table. The big one was Third Bass on 52nd Street. It was owned by Gus Lacey. People used to call him Mr. Silk because he wore these bad ass silk suits. I mean he walked in the place bladed down" she recalled.

"Oh yeah mama! I remember the Mamma Jamma. Wasn't that on 52nd Street? It was a cheese steak place, wasn't it?" I asked.

"Yep. Foo Foo Regan had it. It was right down the street from Third Bass. I'm surprised you remember that. The big Cabaret places in West Philly were the Imperial Ballroom, the Orchard Room and the Adelphia House" she said.

"What about South Philly? Did you get down there much?" I asked.

"Oh yeah. South Philly was rough and ready. People didn't shoot each other in those days, but they would knife you in a minute. It was worse than North Philly, especially

before the riots. South Philly had several spots. We had Budweiser at 16th and South
and the Postal Card down the Street. Showboat had live features. It was on 15th Street.
Now on 16th Street from Christian to Fitzwater we had Emerson's, Sims Paradise and
the Two Bit Club. A man named Coatesville Harris had a place called Spider Kelly over
on Mole Street. Oh and how can I forget Peps? Peps was the spot right there at Broad
and South. I mean that place used to jump! I don't remember too many cabarets. They
may have had them, but I'm not too sure. It didn't matter. We had it. That's why I don't
care nothing about this high tech digital, dot com fritter or whatever the hell it is going
on now. It'll never come close to the good times we had" she said.

"That's twitter mom, not fritter" I replied.

"What sunever you call it. These people out here are confused and stressed. That
mess is what sets people nuts! My gang was not stressed."

"Mom, finish telling me about the hot nights at the dance" I insisted.

"The dance hall held about two, maybe three hundred people. Everybody had a
table filled with their people. Say this is my table. I have my sister and her husband
and my girlfriend and her husband and so on. The table was loaded down with pots
of greens, chitterlings, ribs, hot sauce and cheap liquor. The music was bouncing and
the dance floor was loaded. I tell you it really was a good time. The women checked
out every woman coming in the door. Some women gave a hard stare. We called it
grittin. They would grit her from the bottom of her feet to the top of her head and
then start picking her apart. They watched who she came there with, whose table she
was with."

"What was all of that grittin for Mama? Did they know the woman?"

"Sometimes. It usually happened when a woman looked really good and the other
men, especially their man, was looking at her or they knew the wife or girlfriend of the
man she came in with. Worse yet, the wife's or girlfriend's family may be there. Other
times it was people who had a long standing fight going and they weren't but a minute
off from each other anyway. Anything could get it going."

"Aw sookie sookie now! Would that lead to a fight?"

"Before the night was over somebody was gonna have something to say. Sooner
or later some woman started running her mouth saying something about somebody's
family member or friend or called somebody a bitch at another other table. They would
start signifying; 'will you look at that head? Some people think they're so cute. They
need to go home and take that raggedy assed dress with'em!' And you know how that's
gonna turn out."

I jumped up on mom imitating what I imagined took place. "I know you ain't talking
about my sister! You got something to say, dammit, say it to my face!" I yelled.

Mom continued cracking up laughing "You know that's right. Then here comes the
other sister and their cousin getting in it to defend her. Then somebody from another table
gonna get in it. Next thing you know chairs and tables were flying. Potato salad was on
the floor. A couple of times somebody got clucked upside the head with a whisky bottle
and blood flew. People were moving out of the way. 'Give'em room y'all' somebody

might holler. Then a woman stepped on another woman's toe on the dance floor and you remember those roach killer shoes we wore back in the day."

"What, you can't see me bitch?" I mocked.

"And that's all it took. It was never one on one. At least six or seven people had to get in it and tear each other apart. Once in a while somebody called the cops, but for the most part it was every man for himself. I remember one night at the Imperial Ballroom two women were on the floor tearing each other up. I didn't know either of them. One woman ripped up the other woman's dress. Nobody pulled them apart at first. People loved to see a good fight. One was just as bad as the other. After they damn near killed each other, then some people came in and broke it up. They were torn up" she said.

"What's happening with the rest of the dance during this time? Was the party over, huh? Did the music stop?" I wondered.

"No indeed. All the time folks were fighting and carrying on the music kept going and people kept dancing. The band was paid to play until two in the morning and that's what they did. After a while the fight cooled off and the people who were fighting left and that was that. Afterward everybody had something to say about it."

"Oh I can hear it now mama. She needs to mind her business. What was she doing all up in it anyway? I don't know why she was mad. She always got so much to say about everybody else. She needed to get her ass kicked. I can't stand her my damn self" I mocked again.

"Yea, yea that's it! You know the talk. Whoever couldn't make it to the dance had an earful. Girl you missed it! Then they'd run down who was fighting, how it got started and the mess that was left behind. These were public dances that cost about two fifty, maybe three dollars to get in. When social organizations started having their affairs, they sold tickets through club members, not at the door. They had to cut out that fussing, fighting and confusion."

"I'm thinking about that song by Garret Mimms. Remember *Quiet Place*?"

Mom and I sang together "*I can't get no sleep in this noisy street, I got to move, got to find me a quiet place.*"

Slowly black folks were starting to find a quiet place by moving from North Philadelphia and West Philly, to West Oak Lane, Mount Airy and parts of Germantown. North Philly had gone crazy by now with gang war and riots. The Morocco's, Tenderloins, Cubana, The Valley, Diamond Street and De Marco were gangs of North Philly. The Moon and The Creek had West Philly. Break-ins and spontaneous fires were more frequent. Anyone who had a good job or just hit the street number moved out. Blacks were up from the bottom and were starting to live in unfamiliar parts of Philly. Nobody knew the difference between Mount Airy and Fox Chase.

1966

Two years before The Equal Housing Bill was passed in D.C. black folks wasted no time in trying to take advantage of it so they could begin to live better lives. Armed with the Civil Rights Bill, Voting Rights Act and legal integration of schools, Negroes sought to empower themselves politically, socially and economically. Blockbusting helped to improve living status and scared white folks clean out of their homes. After one black family moved in, the tone was set. Whites didn't want blacks overcoming next to them. As soon as they saw their new neighbor was of color, realtors were hard at work assuring them property values were going down and trouble was sure to come in a *changing* neighborhood. It was called black blight and white flight. Many whites became angry because they were comfortable in their homes raising their families. They thought they were free from tension and trouble. Now they had to find a way to get some money and move out. Their anger was reflected in many newspapers across Philadelphia. My parent's friends talked about going to bed Friday night with white neighbors and waking up Saturday to black ones. They never saw for sale signs displayed, never heard or saw a truck back up, they just disappeared. Realtors must have cleaned out North Philly. A dollar down and a dollar when you catch me was all that was needed and the house was sold with anxious owners ready to move to the northeast and the outskirts of town. Most blacks never thought about what they were running into, only what they were running from.

Once the trailblazers settled in, they gave parties to show the house off and had to give directions on how to get to there. These *new* houses had air-conditioning, wall to wall carpet, garbage disposals, dishwashers and a second bathroom. Ladies talked about their new vacuum cleaners with attachments and eye level stoves. Cellars were finished basements and the elite had a recreation room with a small bathroom called the powder room. A garage was in the back and a patio in the front. Porches were passé. For the first time many had automatic washers and dryers. Thick slat blinds were out. Shades with custom drapes were a must. And please no more ceiling lights in the living room. Appliances came in modern colors of avocado and bronze. Some had a combination in the living room that never worked for long and an eight track component set. The party began with the hostess giving a tour of her beautiful home. The house tour came with a narrative for every room. Their diction had a quasi-dialect only the arrivals could acquire. They couldn't say peas for the pod. Ladies delicately batted their eyes while mentioning their Van Schivers account where they bought their Armoire and dressing tables that replaced Chester and bureau drawers. The house tour ended with a view of the king size bed and walk in closets with lights. These well to do women secretly had their tongues stuck to the roof of their mouths from licking S&H green stamps.

These new and classy arrivals were owned by their coupon book. Mortgage row didn't have regular house parties. The first thing they did was to stop eating chitterlings, collard greens, fried chicken and barbeque ribs. It was considered tacky and greasy. No more hanging at the beer garden or carrying greasy paper bags with cheap liquor on the table. Fancy liquor cases, and later, an open bar became standard and top shelf liquor was required. They had cocktails and coasters. The hostess would make a tray load of martinis with a little olive floating on top. A fifth of liquor could serve a house full of people. The new facade was complete with the hostess gown, the rise from Avon to French perfume, finger food complete with the chafing dish, a champagne fountain and their good Bone china. They required decanters and carafes, cocktail forks and toothpicks, candles burning in crystal hurricane holders and cloth napkins. A sterling silver ice bucket with a five foot stand was placed on the floor at the end of the linen covered table. This was all under the shadow of a crystal chandelier dimmed to a romantic glow perfect for classy mingling. They had come a long way from having an ice bucket on the table.

The menu included clam dip, caviar, shrimp, and clams casino, pigs in a blanket, oysters Rockefeller, and mushrooms stuffed with crab meat. And it was all catered, of course. Long gowns were blowing and flowing across a deep shag carpet toting a cocktail in one hand and a cigarette in the other, sporting a midwinter tan giving all the details of their recent trip to the islands that was written up in the Tribune's Society Section, better known as the Black Dispatch. Their conversations were filled with the latest trip to Nassau, Freeport or Port au Prince, Haiti. They sent post cards making sure everyone knew where they were. Every post card I ever saw ended the same; Wish *You Were Here*. To fly anywhere was notable. It was the first time for many. They quickly became known as Jet Setters known for wearing their best attire for travel. Ladies shopped all week to find just the right outfit for airport day. She wore a beautiful dress or a suit with hat and gloves. Men wore a sports suit and by the early seventies a Leisure suit. They went through a roll of film just to get to the gate. The in-crowd boasted about their matching Samsonite luggage and the privileged services from the sky cap and stewardess. No children were in the curtained off first class section. They basked in swivel chair luxury and personal service. In those days passengers received a hot meal, drinks and a fashion show. If the right crowd was on board strangers became friends and the party began thirty seven thousand feet in the air.

Two and three outfits were required per day—one for each meal. It meant a lot to be seen. If anyone didn't keep up they were fodder for egos. The social agenda meant that ladies crossed their legs at the ankle and never be seen twice wearing the same outfit.

They sipped drinks lightly with a pinky salute. Beer was in very poor taste. Scotch was the order of the day. Having seconds on anything was rude unless it was offered.

Splash Parties were en vogue at the Black owned Nile Swim Club in Yeadon. The Green Briar Country Club in Winfield Heights and the Woodford Tennis Club were arrival statements for the growing middle class. It was an exclusive establishment that excluded every ethnic group, even Jewish people, but now because of the movement the doors opened. Pool parties were just like the beach parties. Nobody got wet, except for maybe sitting on the edge and dipping their feet. No one was about to get the sequin and rhinestone bathing suit wet. It was mostly sipping cocktails and basking in the moment of status, be it real or imagined. The hustle of catching planes and hotel check-ins lay in stark contrast to bus terminals and long hot car rides. Until that time it was just an annual trip down south or to Chicken Bone Beach. So if any black person says they were in Vegas back in the day they're a damn lie.

Cloud Nine

Negroes tried to be proud of blackness, but some put it down at the same time. Fatback music along with the fat back was low class and looked down upon. The so called "Chitlin Circuit" was abandoned. They didn't dare grub on the grease in the open and it seemed everyone forgot what an outhouse was. Nobody admitted to having ever done a days work, emptying slop jars or had a clue to the hard times. They forgot about the days when they were down in Virginia or Georgia with chicken shit squeezed between their toes. They talked and acted as if they'd always had it going on. Most didn't even get over the Great Depression until the mid to late fifties.

Now Chevy's and Ford's were for poor struggling people. Cadillac's were for those who had arrived. Cloth coats were pushed to the back of the closet to make room for silk mohair and mink stoles.

Arrival. The word alone brought the right to dream and a reason to strive. It brought feelings of resentment and envy. I meant children going to prestigious colleges. It meant a large income—not wealth. It was defined by how much certain people had and what they could buy. It never occurred to some that while having a good job was indeed progress and was a long time coming, that Negroes didn't and still don't own or control anything at a level that affects Wall Street. As a people we still depended on others to buy our labor. The progress that was made was phenomenal, but it really just got us to the starting line—late. Some of our sisters and brothers totally forgot that part. The new Negro diverted into two groups.

Is that black enough for ya!

The first group was usually over thirty and hung up on cars, mink coats, houses, diamonds, vacations and wardrobe. They had Roosevelt's New Deal mentality and took to European tradition. Their goal was *the man's* goal. European cuisine and décor were the only decent symbols of the progressive crowd. They had to have separate glassware for each category of alcohol and large mahogany book shelves loaded down with Shakespeare, Poe and some other people I never heard of leaving the house virtually devoid of anything Negroid. A few got to the point they couldn't even pray in church like they used to. Hard sanctified gospel that made you holler service disappeared into polite arias, peaceful prayers and controlled praise. Some blacks removed themselves from the Baptist faith altogether, becoming the more refined Methodist, Presbyterian and Catholic. Wardrobe and impressions upstaged the Sunday text. Hard to praise and impress. It was through the power of those "slap your mama" churches that we had the new life to begin with. What used to be the heart of survival and the cradle that birthed the movement gave way to fanfare and profiling. Purging, cleansing and renewal of heart and spirit were overshadowed by self absorbing facades. Here is a crowd that got brand new when, less than ten years earlier, the only hors d'oeuvre they had were deviled eggs and pickled pigs feet. They didn't have martini glasses; they had paper cups and jelly jars filled not with cocktails, but hard ass liquor and it was sometimes bootleg at that. It's okay to get further and smell better, that's what it's all about, but some acted as if it were a matter of course. Many were labeled as snooty, phony and snobby by their peers and were called programmed by young, proud Afro-Americans.

Soul Sister #1

The second group was the under thirty crowd into black power and proud of nappy hair. They embraced African art; had an Angela Davis portrait, ultra mod décor, red, black and green somewhere in the house and their book collection included W.E.B Dubois and James Baldwin. They had no time for the Duke or the Count anymore. Louis Armstrong was now a shameful throw back of the Shine era. They talked about the new social order where traditions of marriage and women in the kitchen were over and looked toward black men to be front and center. They spoke of their views on conspiracies behind assassinations. The new Massa was the F.B.I. and the new plantation was every ghetto and prison in America. Some chair-back intellectuals tried to mimic the big heads of the day. They adopted philosophies on what everyone needed to do to get their program together—resisting that psyche job the white man was putting down and promoting the birth right of divinity from the motherland.

Stokely Carmichael was an activist during the Civil Rights Movement. Years of protest and marches filled him with fever for empowerment for black people. He said we had to stop worrying about the other man and get ourselves straight. We needed self determination by defining one's own culture and controlling one's own path. That's what Black Power was supposed to mean. It was spoken to hearts broken from oppression and weary from limitations. Status quo had successfully manipulated equal rights into special treatment or special threat. Politicians didn't kiss black babies or shake black hands. No particular attention was paid until we were either too successful or too angry. Both were shut down with brutal precision and notables were taunted with death threats and untimely shut downs. Anybody who wanted to help poor people seemed to end up dead. Anyone who made that connection was a conspiracy theorist, a cynical person who was never creditable.

H. Rap Brown shouted for black folks to stand up. Stokely said wake up. Dr. King said sit down. Malcolm told us about the blue eyed devil. White folks said step back, black folks said step up and the rest of us were caught in the middle. Wanting to be apart of the democratic system wasn't the same as overthrowing it. It's possibly too much to process for the conservative mind. Women allegedly burned bras and the antiestablishment population brought drugs, sex and the Vietnam War to the forefront. I wasn't ever bored. It brought energizing conversation everywhere. It filled the newspapers and television. Some people were angry, others whispered their opposing view and I was sent upstairs where I clearly heard almost every word.

If you don't dig it, ig it!

That's right. If you don't get it, ignore it. If you don't like it lump it, then take it to City Hall and dump it. That was the new attitude with blacks feeling and living the result of the revolution movement. There was an important awakening, a redemptive type of arrogance that solidified defiance necessary for the movement. If it wasn't for that, we wouldn't have made it to the starting line yet. We could tell the whole world to go to hell, cuss Charlie out, have his woman and say exactly what was on our mind, and show our ass without as much fear as before. Despite racism people became weary of social protocol, limitations, expectations and restrictions. People thought they were killing white supremacy, not knowing it has a chameleon capability—mutating and disguising as needed. Generational wisdom, known as the old school was dismissed as old fashion and it deprived future generations of spiritual maintenance needed to sustain themselves. Our point of reference eroded. Unacceptable behavior became acceptable in the name of self-determination. Freedom and equality was more elusive than anyone dared to think. The illusion of power and success bred complacency.

"I was with the West Philly crowd. They had a group called the West Set. We had a good time and it didn't cost a lot of money. There wasn't any such thing as cover charge or paying for parking. And after the 2 A.M. shut down in Philly, Jersey was the place to go. That's when we used to say we were going down the Ridge and over the Bridge. We ended up in Merchantville to Over the Top; we had Brady's Dream Land, Lauretta's High Hat and The Dew Drop Inn. Those were the best places to party. Segregation didn't matter, the white man didn't matter. We had it right there. Barbeque sauce and liquor were flying. We carried on until morning and everybody made it home in one piece. Soul food and a bottle of whiskey in grease spotted brown paper bags were on every table. The band burned up and was threatening every crack in the ceiling with a roaring crowd. People partied all night long and for a while there wasn't any violence."

The Latin Casino

Ben and Hazel Lyons at the Latin Casino, 1967

1964 at Orchid Ballroom

Not a day went by that I didn't hear people singing We Shall Overcome or see them dancing to *Green Onions* at the same time. I heard mom and dad talk with friends about whites in the south who didn't want black children to go to *their* school. They knocked black folks upside the head just because they could. Those who stood up were as good as dead. Dad said to mom that if the schools were indeed equal, maybe there wouldn't be so much fuss. Equality would have to come with the stipulation of black schools having plumbing and heat; ceilings that didn't leak and school books that weren't tattered. They needed lunchrooms and sports equipment just like the white schools. Who'd care about integration if those conditions had been met?

Churches and homes were bombed and children were killed. In modern times people were afraid to try to register to vote or sign a petition. In doing so, they could be out of a job, a home or dead. No one was on the street alone after dark. Television was filled with blood and gore and people were getting angrier. Philadelphia was becoming a police state. The Man, mostly white policemen, could beat and kill with no threat of indictment. I was too young to understand the troubles around me, but old enough to feel the anger and despair that haunted the grown-ups in my life.

Sweet Sixteen Bars

We just finished dinner. Mom put the dishes in soak and the evening news with Brinkley and Huntley was about to end; Good night Chet—Good night Dave. The TV was turned off and the Hi-Fi tubes were warming up. Flexible notes floated in the air and gently introduced my tender ears to the world of music. Those notes tantalized my soul. I was just as fascinated by the album covers as I was of the music. I was struck by the sunrays hitting the sweat on a wine bottle along with the beautiful brown skinned lady lying on satin pillows. Each cover displayed a unique work of art that took me on imaginary excursions every time my dad shared his collection with me.

Too young to read, I began to associate the album cover with the music I heard. Strayhorn and Brubeck invited my curious mind to listen and discover the power of chords from one stroke of a key. The piano capturing melody and lyric spoke a language I automatically understood. I felt as beautiful as the melody. I was almost in a trance listening and still intrigued by the cover it came in. I didn't realize a smile came across my face while my toes spontaneously tapped in the air. Dad strummed with the record on his hollow box guitar. I was drawing it in. I was struck by how he could hit the same note at the same time as the record. I wasn't moved to dance. I discovered the gift of listening. Mom came into our empty dining room where dad was playing the same chords again. I knew them this time. Then mom put words to those chords. She looked at me and smiled. Then she began to sing:

> She wished me blue birds in the spring,
> She wished me a song to sing,
> She wished me health, much more than wealth,

She wished me love. Dad barely flexed his right hand with a pick and crimped his left hand on the fret. I heard two notes at the same time. I almost saw the quarter note he created. One finger made the most beautiful sound—mommy's gentle intonation made me feel like a star. She looked at dad and continued her song:

> She wished him shelter from the storm,
> A cozy fire to keep him warm,

Dad stopped playing and mom paused for a moment. They looked at each other and together sang:

> But most of all—when snowflakes fall—I wish you love.

Ain't Nobody here but us Chickens

I would often awake with a song in my head. The spell wasn't broken until mom hurried me off to school for a half day of kindergarten at Add B. Anderson School on Cobbs Creek Parkway. Mom was in the schoolyard at the end of my half day to walk me home. It was an especially stormy day. I had to wear low cut boots called rubbers and my raincoat. I couldn't wait to get in out from the weather. Mom quickly resumed the chores she had already begun that morning. Mom was on her knees with a red brush painting the oven with Easy-Off while I enjoyed Romper Room and Wee Willy Weber. Top Cat and Etch-a-Sketch filled my day. We had a box on our TV for UHF. Mom took a break to sip her cup of instant coffee and made a Skippy peanut butter sandwich with Bond bread for me. She never missed *Concentration* with Hugh Downs or the old *Jeopardy!,* hosted by Art Fleming on channel 17. While the Easy Off soaked the oven clean, mom took a break and spent time with me reading, playing with my dolls or my puzzles. She told me stories about when she was a little girl just like me. She taught me her schoolyard rhymes and classroom songs to help me get through cloudy days.

I tried to see through the teardrops the sky left on the windows. The trees were nothing more than naked logs pointing toward dismal clouds that defied my beloved sunshine. Mom turned the television off and turned the radio on. I watched mom meticulously dust the leather top mahogany drum table. She asked me to turn on the ceiling light to hold back the gloom. With a different cloth she polished the claws with black oil. She had washed all of the knick knacks in ammonia spiked dishwater and placed everything perfectly in place. On her hands and knees I watched her clean the baseboards and scratch every speck of dust out from hidden corners. She rolled the tank vacuum across the floor and began to attack the sofa cushions. She fluffed them up and squeezed them tight into place. When she finished the quiet in the room was louder than before she began. She saw me watching her. She smiled, but didn't miss a beat until she was satisfied with our polished palace. She began to sing with a song on the radio as usual, but I wasn't particularly stirred. When she returned the vacuum to the closet, she pulled out a brown case. I had always wondered what was in there.

"I want you to hear something. I think you'll like it" Mom said and looked at me as if she saw my isolation.

"These are songs people enjoyed long before they had television. I loved to listen to them when I was a young girl. Music was all I had" she went on.

She opened the box. There were records inside she called 78s. They were shellac records that felt almost like glass. They were bigger than the 45s, but smaller than rubbery albums. They didn't have the colorful jackets like daddy's albums. They were just boring brown paper. The box was filled with recordings by people I never heard of. Mom soon changed that. She went to the hi-fi and flipped the needle backwards. Then she changed the speed on the turntable. I heard it fly in circles. The intro sounded funny at first, but I saw mom enjoying it so much. She had that smile that told me it had to be right.

The buzzard took the monkey for a ride in the air . . .

"That's Nat King Cole sweetheart! Man how we used to turn it out on this one. He was so smooth. White women went nuts over him!" she declared.

She sang the song all the way through. I loved it. I knew half the words when she played it again. *Just Can't See for Lookin* was on the other side. She took that one off and put on Louis Jordan. She played *Knock me a Kiss* and *Ain't Nobody here but us Chickens*. I learned every word of the old school rap. I began to look forward to those 78s, the first oldies I knew. She played *Whispering Grass*. The Ink Spots song warned the grass to stop telling secrets to the trees who told the breeze then the birds and bees. Now everybody knows the secrets from under the trees. Those blabbering trees sounded just like the blabbering porch ladies. I had that tune in my head every time I heard one of them with a mouth full of somebody else's business.

Mom put another record on. I finally heard her. Mom's favorite. Billie Holiday. Her voice was haunting. It pleaded for mercy and raged with fire and pain. She soulfully sang just behind the beat. Her lyric was filled with self possession tinged with dejection. Mom played her again. We both sat on the sofa watching the tears fall from the sky and listened. She sat in a chair and reflected the day, gloomy everywhere. She went right through my body. She knew how I felt and maybe mom did too. Her *Solitude* was also ours. The pop and scratch from the record broke my trance. Mom flipped through the box and pulled another one out. Then she got up and tended to the hi-fi then went into the kitchen. I heard mom sing every word.

Every time it rains it rains . . . pennies from heaven . . .

Billie's voice was a little lighter. She seemed cheerful, but it still had that longing. She turned the clouds into my future and the teardrops on the window were pennies that I can catch if my umbrella was upside down. My mood was altered by the power of music. Just one note brought joy or sorrow. It sent a message and brought an internal comfort that words could not. All of my life music was there to soothe me.

Mom often told me there's nothing in life I will experience that someone didn't sing a song for. That's what good music does. It tells a story. When you're feeling down, keep a song in your heart and sing your blues away, rejoice in the gift that music brings. Allow its power to soothe and heal your soul.

1967

Say it Loud, I'm black and I'm proud

Before conglomerates neutralized our airwaves, radio was an open forum. The radio kept people up on perspectives and opinions that were ignored in other media. There weren't as many commercials or the same songs played over and over again, but rather announcements of events, rallies and who's coming to the Uptown. Located at Broad and Susquehanna, it was an oasis of talent and relief from troubles. In spite of frightening turbulence, despair gave way to hope for a better day. Motown gave us The Miracles, The Supremes and The Impressions. WDAS radio was the sanctuary of soul and awareness. It was where black people could depend on being heard and understood. Lord Fauntleroy was the first Deejay I remember. We had Donny 'Gold finger' Brooks, Jocko and Carl Helm who told us what we needed to know. Georgie Woods owned his microphone. He had people dancing and thinking at the same time. Sometimes he played the same song twice. Then he'd stopped the sounds whenever he wanted to make a relevant argument or recite some history. Then he opened the phone lines on the spot and debated with civic leaders or the general public about any headway or set back for the city. Then he got back to jamming Power-to-the-People! Everyday People! People Get Ready! Most soul music was recorded on independent labels that began to put jazz music in the back seat—almost the grave. *Stax, Chess, Soul* and *King* Records fueled the revolution, the movement and the people. It was the heart of house parties and cabarets, riots and demonstrations, love and lust, blood and violence, quest for freedom and education and an overall we-ism never seen since.

The Revolution has Come!

The Black Panther Party hit the newspapers sometime in 1967 and at first nobody knew what they were about. The porch ladies were scared of them. They wore black leather jackets and only came out at night. It had me scared. I wasn't sure if they were talking about people or cats. People said they were for the people. Television said they were a troublesome gang that had to be stopped. Hoover said they were public enemy number one. But their slogan was Power to the People—all oppressed people. Later, the word was they tried to enlighten black people that everyone else forgot about. They taught people about their rights and protected citizens from police brutality. Land, bread, housing, education, clothing, justice and peace for everyone was their plea. They fed more hungry children than the U.S. government and raised bail for those who were arrested. They challenged the status quo and raised conscious levels. They spoke truth to power. That's what couldn't be tolerated. They were out of their place, but they also scared too many people. Sometime during their mission, FBI counterintelligence successfully divided and conquered the party. Their quest to raise the conscience level of poor blacks was lost when they acquired a siege agenda and fell out of favor with too many black people. The progressive crowd didn't take too well to the Black Panthers or young black men in black leather jackets. They distanced themselves from poor peoples' struggle. After all, middle class Negroes were no longer oppressed or so they thought. They gravitated toward Dr. King who was a warrior for education, personal responsibility and assimilation into mainstream as a means of getting ahead. They shunned anything radical. They didn't wear afros or dashikis. They didn't even holler Right On! They had just enough and they had too much to loose. Their new zip code and phone number exchange had clout. No one was putting it on the crap table.

My family moved from Cecil Street in West Philly to Mount Airy in the summer of 1967. James Brown's *Cold Sweat*, *Ode to Billie Joe* by Bobbie Gentry and *When Something is Wrong with my Baby* by Sam and Dave were the number one hits. It was the year before Dr. King was assassinated, but in the events leading up to that day, life was uncertain. Nothing was predictable. There were upsets and demonstrations all over. Police and college students were hostile. Police and demonstrators were hostile. Police in black neighborhoods meant harassment and trouble. Public schools were slowly integrating. Many black people took their children out of public school and put them into catholic school to protect them from the ever increasing mayhem. The F.B.I. declared just about every organization in the United States as radical or otherwise a threat to the security of the country.

Pantry Pride

Mount Airy was mostly a Jewish area with just a few block busting Negroes. Where Martin Luther King High School now sits used to be a row of homes with a bar on the corner and it was all white. My parents spent the rest of the summer getting familiar with our new neighborhood. Ogontz and Stenton Avenues were lined with shops and restaurants. The Stenton Diner was located near Washington Lane and was a Sunday dinner favorite. Cedarbrook was our first mall experience. It had the new supermarket, Pantry Pride. Cheltenham Square was an open shopping center. Cemeteries were still segregated. African Americans still buried loved ones in Mount Lawn or Eden cemeteries. Chelten Hills and Ivy Hill cemeteries were off limits. Ogontz Avenue was alive with the Renel Theater and the present day Senior Center was the Five and Dime Store, also known as the 5&10.

The few blacks there were a completely different crop from the West Philly crowd. Mount Airy ladies varied from housewives to professionals. They hung their clothes on the line in the Back Bay and always seemed to have a broom in their hand. Children were well behaved, neat and clean and played nicely. The air was filled with pride and care. Grass was watered daily and clipped religiously. The streets were spotless. The few professional women were Cheney or Howard alumni. Some had their own car and were never seen without their make-up. A few of them had cleaning ladies. While everyone was neighborly, some distanced themselves from one another. I didn't see any porch ladies and I kinda missed them. They were not running in and out of other peoples houses. No music blared in the street. Nobody hung their head out of the window.

We had colored neighbors on both sides of our house that moved in just months prior to us. Ms. Lucille was peacock proud and much younger than my mother. She and her husband were both college grads and were "brand new". She was black and proud with a blow-out fro to prove it. She claimed that most Negroes "weren't ready" for the new black awareness movement; going back to the Mother Land, the politics of B-Afra and support of the Black Liberation Army. Ms. Lucille and her husband Sterling, the Kathleen and Eldridge Cleaver of the block, were self appointed trend setters for the neighborhood. Mom listened, but never went along with any of it. She figured after fussing and fighting about it, nothing would change anyway. She did manage to give mom some African literacy and mom offered her some old school care she never had. Most neighbors distanced themselves from the radical movement. They didn't want any noise about anything. Except for a precious few, usually the under thirty crowd, no one wore an afro or dashiki, talked about black power or burned incense. They did talk about the changes that were all about us, but had a more conservative approach. They wanted to live nicely, quietly and send their children to good schools. They were sort of like the housekeeper in the white folk's kitchen who went to a rally last night, but answered the mister with profound disgust when asked what they thought about the radical movement.

Miss Mary Mack . . . .

My first summer in my new home gave me a back bay and driveway to play in. It was a lot bigger than the front porch, which I would've preferred. I began to play with some of the little white children and became friends with most of them. Their whiteness never crossed my mind until a couple of them offered me candy and later accused me of stealing it and owing them sixty-five cents—a lot of money. It was ugly after my parents came to my defense and their parents came to theirs. Mom tried to keep the real problem out of my ears. However I did hear the woman shout through the window "I wish you'd go back to Columbia Avenue where you came from!" I stood there wondering what she meant. Columbia Avenue was that fighting street—a long way from us. What was she so angry about? It was the first of many lessons I was learning, one of which was that I was a colored child and what that meant. I was too confused to be hurt. Sometimes I was shocked because I heard my mother talk in a totally different tone than I was ever used to. She allowed me to play with the children after that, but told me under no uncertain terms that I was to never accept anything from them. She made sure I had my own bubble gum and licorice.

Black families trickled in during the summer, but I only paid attention to the ones that had kids I could play with. Two girls just my age liked to play house with their dolls. We made mud pies and pretended to make collard greens with maple tree leaves. Sometimes I stole a little flour from the kitchen and mixed it with water to make mashed potatoes. Two little girls who happened to be white came out of their home about five houses down. They saw us about the same time we saw them. Their smile led us to think we were about to have new friends, but instead they greeted us with "Niggers, ooh look at the niggers!" I stopped mixing my potatoes to look at my friends who returned the same befuddled look. What could we do, or say? What was that for? Why were they looking at us? I had no idea what it all meant, but had the feeling they didn't want to play with us. I was again confused because other white children didn't appear that way at all. They wanted to play just like me. They were playful and we shared our candy. Certain ones made it clear that I was dirty, that I was stinky and wasn't fit to be with. What were they talking about? Mommy gave me a bath every night with Lifebuoy soap and sometimes with Mr. Bubbles. I became leery of those who were nice because I didn't want to take the chance. I never knew when they may turn mean.

I started Pennypacker Elementary School in West Oak Lane in the fall of 1967. Every outfit my mother had for me required a stiff starch shirt with tiny buttons and puff sleeves with peter pan collars. Wrangler jeans and sneakers were never allowed. My chestnut brown hair was in braids that barely made it to my neck with little barrettes that kept them respectable. Fifth and sixth grade boys were crossing guards who proudly got the little ones to and from school safely. They wore their safety strap and monitored the corner. When traffic came they straddled their legs and held their arms out. When all was clear they stepped to the side and allowed us to pass. No one harassed him. He had status that was honored and always respected. If anyone stepped out of line they were reported to the teacher who in turn called their parents. I cannot imagine such a level of sensibility today among our technically savvy populace. Students, parents or administrators would soon propose a problem.

I was one of three Negro children in a classroom with an old lift top desk and chair connected. An ink well was on the top right of the desk. My first grade teacher, Mrs. Moss was an older white woman with bluish white hair and pointy bifocal glasses. I couldn't tell when she smiled or frowned. She was a surrogate parent who kept cumulus clouds looming. Discipline wasn't ever a problem except for a slapping ruler on the desk of a sleeping child. It happened to me three times. She divided up the class in three sections; the red birds, the yellow birds and the blue birds. I was a blue bird. We started each day with prayer, a pledge to the flag and round America the Beautiful.

My classmates had names I never heard before; Galpstein, Edelberg and Moskovitz. The holy days of Yom Kippur and Rosh Hashanah gave them school free days the rest of us didn't have. After placing our right hand over our hearts to take our daily pledge, we began our lessons for the day. Mrs. Moss read to the class daily and had the class read aloud. My favorite author was Dr. Seuss and my favorite book was Madeline. We were anxious to make friends during recess. Girls and boys segregated themselves—each not liking the other, but there wasn't ever a fight. I walked home from school for lunch down the now familiar driveway. On any given day sheets and draws were blowing in the crisp air that smelled of Argo starch tinged with a hot lunch. I sat down to a hot bowl of chicken and stars soup and a grilled cheese sandwich. Vince Leonard was head anchor on Eyewitness News. Mom sacrificed the Mike Douglass show so I could watch Pixanne before making my way back to school. I had a turn of hopscotch at afternoon recess just before that irritating bell rang. Like marching ants, we had to make a straight line on the painted schoolyard before our lock step march back to class. Afternoons zipped by with coloring books, arithmetic, phonics and spelling bees. She settled us down with a short story and sent us to the cloak room in sections to get out jackets for home. The red birds were first, then the yellow birds and finally the blue birds. We were free birds once we hit that schoolyard.

I looked forward to home after school. Mom always had something to eat waiting for me, but I couldn't do anything until I finished my homework. She signed me up for piano lessons at Warner Brothers Pianos located on Ogontz Avenue. My school work kept me busy. My music kept me fulfilled throughout the school year.

As the fall settled in the air so did my anticipation for my first memorable trick-or-treat. Mischief night was a night for spooky movies and popcorn and putting the finishing touches on Halloween costumes. Sometimes mom helped me make mine, which was more fun than buying one. The older kids took advantage of Mischief night by throwing eggs at peoples' windows and vandalizing windshields with soap. Halloween was not considered a pagan holiday. It was a day filled with Popeye, Mickey Mouse and Batman. We were allowed to go to school with our costumes and enjoyed a classroom party. After school and a quick dinner, children dragged their parents on a journey around the neighborhood. We went only to houses that had their front light on, which was almost everyone. Every block was loaded with children of all ages having fun and enjoying treats; candy apples, Reese's cups and ginger snaps. Danger never crossed our mind. My friends and I learned witches were for real. Three ladies, a mother and two daughters who looked more like triplets had Casper white skin and white straw hair. They drove around in a big sky-blue Cadillac. They were always together and spotted at the supermarket and shopping mall. They wore all black and greeted petrified stares with a warm smile. Children went to their house for trick or treat and so did I, but they made me a little nervous. They were called the Witches of West Oak Lane.

Christmas in Mount Airy was the biggest event of the year. After dinner my parents and I jumped into Florence to ride all around town to see the Christmas lights of every color that twinkled in the yuletide spirit and adorned nearly every house from the front lawn to the rooftop. Entire neighborhoods were lit. It was a most beautiful sight. Every neighborhood became an enchanted village of its own. I had my own Enchanted Village at home. Large Christmas bulbs with every color of the rainbow gave the entire block a warm glow, especially if it snowed. With every house lit up and every door open to friends, grown folks did serious party hopping on Christmas Eve from one end of town to another. The children got together on the eve walking up and down every street for blocks around singing Christmas carols and as we went along more people joined in. At the end of the frosty night we ended up at someone's house for hot chocolate and holiday treats. On Christmas day everyone made the rounds to see what everyone else had under their tree. It was open house for the entire twelve days. Black eye peas were still a must for New Years Eve and a man still had to be the first to enter the house on New Years day. Both were for good luck. People kept Christmas lights up two, sometimes three weeks after the New Year. It was just about Valentines Day before the last Christmas ball disappeared and people stopped greeting each other with Happy New Year.

1968

They'll take your soul if you let them . . .

I was six years old when Dr. King was assassinated and totally unaware of his significance, but I remember that day well. School had early dismissal the day after his death. It was a sunny spring day. Class was interrupted by an announcement on the PA system for an unscheduled assembly. We were told of the death of Dr. King and stood to sing *We Shall Overcome*. Afterward we were dismissed from the side doors of the auditorium into the school yard. I saw Mrs. Moss and the principal holding each other and crying on my way out the door—didn't think she had it in her. People were outside talking in huddles, holding handkerchiefs, taking off their glasses and sometimes holding each other. Dads who were normally at work were home. When I got home, my dad was sitting in the kitchen. I knew then something was wrong. Neither television nor the radio was on. They were so sad as if someone in our family died. Mom made him known to me and what he stood for. I'm not sure I knew I was black; pardon me, colored until that time. She explained to me what it meant to be colored, how it is blessed, spiritual and risky in our sick and dangerous society, that I am limited in the freest country of the world. There are people who are fighting for a chance to make America closer to what it said it already was. That was made clear when I saw some of the riots and violence on television. I remembered watching Huntley and Brinkley news during dinner. I remembered those dogs; I remembered the hoses, the fire, mean cops and hatred at its worst. One man I still remember was washed down in blood. He was a white man resting on a telephone poll holding a sign. I saw the fire hose that blew a woman clear off of her feet, cops beating her with the night stick on the ground. Grown people were as helpless as me. I heard the blood chilling cries and screams, the kind that startled the soul, provoking adrenalin and fear. I saw the blood, I saw the smoke and I felt anger and despair. Sometimes I cried all night. I was so upset. I just didn't understand it. I felt the threat come out of the television and punch me in the stomach. I was haunted by those images of blood and savagery. It was not Hollywood, it was America. It was not special effects, it was real. It wasn't a revolution; it was the savagery to our fellow citizens by police. The same authority mom instructed me to seek if I was ever lost or in trouble.

There were people who didn't want all Americans to have a job or to vote. That's what mommy said. The next day in school I pledged allegiance to the flag. Mrs. Moss didn't talk too much about it. She tried to keep our tender minds in a child's place of learning and fun. But in my mind I saw again women and children crying among their dead. I saw soldiers who were in a far away place wounded and bewildered. And the next day I went to school and pledged allegiance to the flag. It was during the Vietnam War that I learned that bodies had parts. I thought it was all one piece. It was during this time I saw blood in the streets, little dead bodies, and people running for their lives while I was singing America the Beautiful. I saw it because the truth, at least at that time, couldn't be hidden. It was the reality of the world. Colored children did not have the luxury of comfort and protection from ugliness. We weren't allowed to have delusions and lies to shield us. Only candy had a sugar coating. I didn't understand how people could be so mean, and for what? Then people have the nerve to tell me that kids are cruel. Through the years mom helped me understand and gave me her wisdom and the teachings of the bible to keep hate out and love in my heart, which doesn't mean being anybody's fool nor to grow bitter, but to be aware and on guard. It meant to make a liar out of those who sought to degrade and belittle, to never indulge in useless anger because it would only harm me. She told me the best way to get to anyone, black or white was to ignore them and succeed on my own path. Just like that Louis Jordan record mama used to play; *You run your Mouth and I'll run My Business*. What others say and think really mean nothing at all. It is only through the process of living that this state of mind can be achieved. She gave me the love and stability every child needs to keep them strong and sustainable in their own right. She opened my mind, told me to use it and own it by giving me instruction, real stories from years gone by, exposures, sharing of her wisdom and the written word as tools and fertile ground to critically think for myself and to never let anyone take that from me.

By second grade there were less white students, but the climate of the school was mostly the same. Most of the colored children were well behaved and were the offspring of the progressive Negro class. Their parents were teachers, owned small businesses and many mothers who had the privilege of not working volunteered at the school. It was called a mixed neighborhood now. Blacks and whites were living side by side in peace. There was hardly ever a fight in school. I began to have friends over to play with dolls for tea parties. Dad took the training wheels off of my red bicycle and I had my first pair of skates. I was well into my piano lessons and hopscotch.

By the time I got to third grade, my class was totally black and too many kids were raising hell. I began to see fights and teachers were beginning to loose control. A demonic force had spun a web. I saw my first fight after school between two boys. One of the boys found a bottle in the street and threw it at the other one. Blood stained the sidewalk. It was more awful than television. Kids were running, screaming and crying. The boy's face was covered with blood diluted with snot and tears. I was stunned. In my desperation to get away, I tripped over someone's school bag and fell. My knees trickled with blood and stained my white knee socks. I had the strange feeling that I was in trouble. Chaos can breed that kind of neurosis. When I got home, mom was standing in the doorway looking troubled. She heard screaming and saw kids running every which way. She patched my knees while I told her what happened. It was bad enough to bring the principal, Mrs. Brown out of her office to address us at assembly the next day. For the first time I heard the words detention, suspension, pink slip and going to the principal's office. School was changing. Students began to back talk the teacher and didn't always have their homework done. A whack with the yardstick was still in practice, but some teachers didn't know how to put meaning behind the stick. Experienced teachers who were older than their birthday and had acquired a piercing eye that cut through your soul. They wore bifocal glasses that made their eyes large and were especially scary. Her eyes were as big as golf balls and there was no mistake about her target. Those eyes pierced through every guilty heart. Her slow and deliberate approach with the sound of her stockings whisking against her fat thighs sounded like a death march closing in. No one wanted to be in that situation. She'd call out to the little incorrigible to stand in the back of the room facing the wall. Talking out of turn earned that punishment. Soon it wasn't enough. It seemed nobody paid attention to the gray eyed gaze anymore.

What a Wonderful World

Going to school, especially on Monday when everyone's scalp was glistening with Sulfur 8 and faces shining with petroleum jelly in the morning sun became the norm. There were no more corn silk pigtails and UFO gazes from blues eyes. Ham sandwich or egg salad sandwiches wrapped in cut-rite wax paper replaced carrot sticks and apples. I began to hear words I didn't understand. Sandwiches became samiches, the iron was the orn, orange was awnge, screens were screams along with strimps, Chicargo, miss-ed, like-ded, drown-ded and such, Old school Ebonics. Some openly chewed gum in class, a vile sin. And the growing popularity of sunflower seeds along with orange peels and seeds made the inside of desks a stinking mess. Borrowing among the students for paper and pencils became a real pain. Milk money, lunch money and school supplies were all at risk. It was the beginning for me of seeing a few children coming to school with bed lint in their uncombed hair, ragged and dirty clothes and coat collars coated with months of Dixie Peach, Glovers Mange and Royal Crown. That I remember. As more black children entered the public schools in what was a prestigious district, the worse the problems came.

The Home and School Association for Pennypacker School hosted a play day and bazaar at the end of every school year. It was a lot of fun with all the classes representing themselves with a dance or some type of fun ritual. There was the cotton candy machine, hot dogs, popcorn, soft pretzels, water ice and other tasty treats for everyone to enjoy with all of the children and their parents meeting and greeting. Special honor was given to the sixth grade graduating class. During the school year the parents and teachers worked together to make the day possible. It was a nice social gathering for both. Around the time of the influx of black and the out flux of whites the quality of the events eroded. Parents and teachers were plagued with disagreements or lack of participation. There was no one left to pick up the slack, white folks were gone. By the end of the next school year, there was no play day or bazaar.

I began to experience teacher's strikes. Weeks of classroom babysitters and no homework infuriated my parents. Pennypacker School had gone from mostly white to mostly black. More fights were breaking out. Classrooms were crowded. Some of my school books were old and tattered. In mid term they snatched me out and put me in private school. Greene Street Friends School was peaceful and filled with black and white students. I was once again readjusting to an environment conducive to learning. For the first time, I began to enjoy school—a little. The message was still penetrating my mind. There was so much going on in my world. At times I was scared of white folks and I was scared of black people too. Without the immediate comfort of my mother I didn't know what to do. Some white kids were hollering nigger and black kids were looking for a fight. They both had me so confused. Everyone was mad. Where does the white perpetration end and our own perpetrations begin I began to wonder? What happened? Who was initiating and who was reacting? We were supposed to be overcoming, proud and determined. Why was it that as soon as some schools and neighborhoods turned black there was this influx of disrespect, inconsideration, trash, cussing and fussing with each other at the very time we needed as much alliance as possible? Then I thought back to the white folks who moved out in such a hurry and had to cease wondering why. Was it necessary to be a pain in everyone's ass? Other people took their children out of public schools and put them into either private academies or Catholic school.

"See, it happened again. I remember when North Philly was white. They lived on Diamond Street, Broad Street and Lehigh Avenues. Strawberry Mansion was all white. Then we had some good Negroes in between. They bought homes and took care of their property. They swept up the street and front steps. Most of their children were well behaved, or at least respectful. C. Percy White was a realtor. Hobson-Reynolds had the Silver Cloud and cruised up and down Ridge Avenue. He was Exalt ruler of the Elks. We had business owners, teachers and lawyers. Some people did days' work and still prospered. It was nice. People left their doors and windows open all summer long. Then it started to turn raggedy. I know the white man didn't do right. We all know it, but that ain't got nothing to do with picking up a broom and taking out the trash. When we first got up here, there wasn't any trash in the street, and no raggedy assed cars in the driveway. We had nice shops on Ogontz and Stenton Avenues and Washington Lane. There was hardly a need for downtown. We had good schools for our children. We didn't have graffiti messing up the walls."

"Don't forget mama, we had some gangs here. Remember the Clang, Rec, Summerville and Haines Street. Some of them used to hang around Simons playground. A couple of the gangs were white and they didn't want the black kids coming to the playground. The little kids were okay, it was the teens that caught it if they were from the wrong side of the fence or the wrong color. That's when people's antennas were getting ripped off because those gangs were making zip guns. There were a lot of cars with coat hangers used for aerials!"

"Yeah. But it was still a nice place to go. I took you there for dance lessons there and went ice skating until your feet got cold! The playground was good for a while. Then fights broke out and I didn't let you go there anymore. That's when you started piano lessons at Warner Brothers on Ogontz Avenue. Then Ogontz went down. Girard Bank left. The Renal Theater had porno movies and the Chinese restaurant had roaches. Raggedy-assed men hung around that liquor store in front of the number six trolley stop. That's what I mean when I say it happened again. This entire area had beautiful homes, shops and schools. That's why people moved. I swear the same termites from North Philly followed us up here and look what happened. Not everywhere and it wasn't everybody but a little is too much. That's part of what tore black folks apart. People trying to have something were called snooty and snobby, and some of that is true, but these snooty people didn't want that trifling element tearing down what they had."

Mom and I went to discuss that most of the residence of Mount Airy, West Oak Lane and Germantown worked and fought hard to keep their homes and neighborhood lovely. Blocks of beautiful tree lined streets were home to beautiful people and kept my world a delightful place to call home.

Girl Talk

Mom was singing every weekend and had to expand her wardrobe. Buying gowns and cocktail outfits were becoming expensive and mom didn't want to be seen in the same gown too many times. Mom's friend Ms. Lillian turned mom on to the best deal of her life; the Thrift Shops. Ms. Lillian used to call them the Junkie Stores. Mom and Ms. Lillian set out for the Junkie Stores. Dad hopped a ride to work so mom could have our car Florence for the day. Ms. Lillian directed mom to the outskirts of Philadelphia known as the Main Line. Route 30 brought us to Narberth, Ardmore and Bryn Mawr where several thrift stores were. Mom found beautiful expensive dresses and gowns at about half the cost. The ladies inspected the expensive material and hand stitched detail. They were elated with a wide variety of sequins, rhinestones and the jewelry to go along with it. Mom saved enough money to expand my wardrobe as well. Racks of clothes were lined with high end store labels ranging from Saks Fifth Avenue, The Blum Store of Philadelphia to Bergdorf Goodman of New York. They tried on shoes and hats. Mom made me try on velvet jump suits and velour play sets. Mom and Ms. Lillian came home with bags of clothes, shoes and odds and ends for the house. Mom was set for her Saturday night gigs now.

Let the Good Times Roll

Mom had several babysitters for me. The Jackie Gleason Show and Swanson TV dinners became my Saturday night treat. The smell of perfume to me meant she was leaving me and I could not go with her. I used to watch her put her make-up on and fix her hair. She took extra care to get her seam straight on the back of her stockings. She took her time fixing herself up just right. She put on the jewelry she bought when we were shopping with her friend Ms. Lillian. Dad packed his guitar in the car and hollered up the stairs for mom to hurry up. They had other people to pick up on their way to the dance. I watched my mom and dad walk out of the front door looking their finest and missing them before the car pulled away from the house.

Each dance brought more music into the house. Dad practiced everyday after dinner on his guitar. He bought sheet music and began to make arrangements. I watched him fill his pen with black or blue in and write every note on music paper. He taught me what B flat looked like on paper then developed my ear on its sound. I had seen written music from my piano lessons, but dad's music sheets seemed complicated. Eight notes and sixteenth just balled my little brain in knots. Dad took time to play piano with me. He taught me how to position my fingers and helped me play my first C major chord. I watched dad learn melodies and make arrangements for the entire band from first and second alto to tenor and sometimes soprano while mom was learning the lyrics. Mom became dad's secretary. She answered the phone and filled in dates while taking care of me and keeping a spotless home.

Tryin' times is what the world is talking about

1968 was one hell of a year. I remembered confusion and upset, but I didn't understand any of America's turmoil. School was closed the day of Dr. King's funeral. Everyone watched it on television. Stores and shops were closed for several days. There was no music in the house. I didn't hear any laughter. Nobody came outside to play. Everything changed. Riots started again. Chicago had a big one. College kids were fighting against the Vietnam War. Mom and dad were upset again when Bobby Kennedy was killed. They said the dream died for sure then. I saw a hippie for the first time in center city and saw a Black Panther on Broad Street. Street gangs had taken neighborhoods over. The *red car* heavily patrolled the streets. Despair and hope shared the same space. People were being killed while others were moving into beautiful homes and traveling to the islands. Life was good, but it was cheap. It was getting better and life was getting worse. Blacks were overcoming and they were declining. Mom held strong to what her grandmother taught her. She never forgot it and made sure I knew as much as she did. It was needed insight for turbulent times and seductive successes. Mom never absorbed what was around her. She didn't become like the porch ladies who rocked their lives away with small petty nonsense. She didn't go along with some of the party ladies who were elegant and became the toast of the social scene, but neglected their families and looked down on other people. She enjoyed everything around her, but she stayed true to her convictions. Empowerment to mom meant not being easily led—not putting too much faith in other peoples' words. It meant not going along with the crowd without a clue as to where the crowd is going. For mom and dad, the good times were just beginning. Their world was expanding into many social elements and so was mine.

Acknowledgements

So many people have helped me on this thoroughfare of literary madness and ecstasy.

My husband Benny McCann helped me very quietly as usual. He never wanted to be noticed, but he was always effective.

The little girls I grew up with are still my hardest loving sisters.

Linda Zabalou who sometimes had the excitement I was too tired to convey offered me her heart and her collection of love and honest sentiment.

Ms. Angie Mobley, my business sister who had the helpful tip or just the lead I needed to carry me a little further.

Caroline and Renee Jordan are the mother daughter team who always left me with that special feeling of it's gonna be alright.

My feisty lady editor Ms. Janet Smith whose wonderful wit helped to keep me focused on finishing the piece. Even after exhaustion had the best of me, she kept my brain engine tuned and geared toward success.

Other special and sincere thanks to Ronald Faulk, Floyd Rudd and Sharon Kraus. Thank you for taking the time from your busy lives to support my attempts to succeed.

Thank you Dr. Charles Blockson for your phone calls of encouragement and enthusiasm.

The staff of Art Noir always welcomed me and turned the art gallery into my second home. It was where I held my very first book signing. Thank you for offering me a place to begin.

My core, the root of everything I have, everything I am comes from the beautiful apple tree I call mama. I never fell too far from her and tried to bear fruit of knowledge and become a bountiful conduit of history, humor and love.

Disease has robbed my father's ability from being a part of my life, but his love and his talents linger in my soul. I cherish my childhood memories and honor the parental essence that gave me a big world filled with a range of understanding and experience during an unforgettable era of revolutionary change.

Their journey continues in the next publication entitled **The Bridge.**